A POCKET GUIDE TO

Writing in History

SIXTH EDITION

Mary Lynn Rampolla

Trinity Washington University

Bedford / St. Martin's   Boston ◆ New York

For Bedford/St. Martin's

Publisher for History: Mary Dougherty
Director of Development for History: Jane Knetzger
Senior Editor: Heidi L. Hood
Developmental Editor: Michelle McSweeney
Production Editor: Lindsay DiGianvittorio
Assistant Production Manager: Joe Ford
Executive Marketing Manager: Jenna Bookin Barry
Text Design: Claire Seng-Niemoeller
Cover Design: Richard DiTomassi
Composition: Karla Goethe, Orchard Wind Graphics
Printing and Binding: Malloy Lithography

President: Joan E. Feinberg
Editorial Director: Denise B. Wydra
Director of Marketing: Karen R. Soeltz
Director of Editing, Design, and Production: Marcia Cohen
Assistant Director of Editing, Design, and Production: Elise S. Kaiser
Managing Editor: Elizabeth M. Schaaf

Library of Congress Control Number: 2009922371

For information, write: Bedford/St. Martin's, 75 Arlington Street, Boston, MA 02116   (617-399-4000)

ISBN-10: 0–312–53503–1
ISBN-13: 978–0–312–53503–2

Acknowledgments

Page 107: From *The Sextants of Beijing: Global Currents in Chinese History* by Joanna Waley-Cohen. Copyright © 1999 by Joanna Waley-Cohen. Used by permission of W. W. Norton & Company, Inc.
Pages 112–13: Copyright © 2008 The Overlook Press / Page 85 from *Scotland: The Autobiography* by Rosemary Goring (Penguin Books, 2007, 2008). Copyright © Rosemary Goring, 2007.

Acknowledgments and copyrights are continued on page viii, which constitutes an extension of the copyright page.

Preface

A Pocket Guide to Writing in History provides a quick reference to the reading, writing, and research skills students need to succeed in their history courses. Though many students in undergraduate courses understand that college writing must do more than restate information gleaned from lectures and books, they may have only a vague idea of how to approach typical history assignments. Instructors, for their part, must convey a great deal of information about history and historical methodology in a limited amount of time, often in large lecture classes; thus, they can devote only very limited time to research and writing instruction. *A Pocket Guide to Writing in History* is designed to aid the instructor and provide guidance for the student in just such situations.

Like the five earlier versions, this new edition of *A Pocket Guide to Writing in History* is comprehensive yet compact enough that it can be tucked into a pocket or backpack. It maintains the most valuable features of earlier versions, providing thorough coverage of the conventions for writing in history—from analyzing an assignment to conducting research, working with written and nonwritten sources, writing effective papers and exams, avoiding plagiarism, documenting sources, and editing for clarity and style. "Tips for Writers" boxes throughout, covering topics such as evaluating sources and avoiding plagiarism, provide easy-to-access checklists of advice. Abundant examples—including sample assignments and sample pages from a research paper—illustrate each step of the research and writing process, and dozens of annotated documentation models based on *The Chicago Manual of Style* show students how to cite print, electronic, and nonwritten sources.

This sixth edition has been revised to make the manual easier to use and give students more practical help with accessing, understanding, writing about, and documenting written and nonwritten sources, both in print and online.

- A new section on single-source analysis assignments in Chapter 3 equips students with in-depth advice on examining and writing about primary sources.

- A new section on distinguishing between popular and scholarly sources in Chapter 2 teaches students this skill critical to conducting academic research.

- Expanded coverage of working with primary sources throughout the text helps students make sense of a wider range of both written and non-written documents.

- Extensive new coverage of online sources in Chapter 5 and elsewhere (including new warnings about *Wikipedia*) explains how to navigate the Internet effectively and helps students understand the sources they find.

- New visual citation guides in Chapter 7—for books, published letters, print articles, database articles, and Web sites—use sample documents to show students where to look for publication information and how to properly cite these common sources.

- Sample note and bibliography models in Chapter 7 have been combined into one section (7c), making it easy for students to find the documentation advice they need for each source they use.

- Additional writing guidance in Chapter 4—including expanded coverage of developing a thesis, a new tip box on revising, more on word choice and active verbs, and new coverage of analyzing and synthesizing sources—helps students craft effective history papers.

- The appendices have been updated to include the most recent and useful indexes, references, periodicals, and Internet sources for student researchers.

In working on this edition, I profited from the advice and encouragement of my colleagues at Trinity Washington University, especially my colleagues in the history program. I owe special thanks to my students, who have offered feedback and suggestions, and whose efforts to become better writers and historians have always inspired me. I am especially indebted to the following historians who reviewed the fifth edition and offered extremely helpful suggestions in preparation for the sixth edition: Heather E. Barry, St. Joseph's College (New York); Getahun Benti, Southern Illinois University–Carbondale; Cornelia H. Dayton, University of Connecticut; Suzanne Desan, University of Wisconsin–Madison; Steven M. Fountain, Washington State University–Vancouver; Karl Friday, University of Georgia; Tami J. Friedman, Brock

University (Ontario); Max G. Geier, Western Oregon University; Rebecca A. Goetz, Rice University; Wesley Gustavson, King's College at the University of Western Ontario; Jessica Harland-Jacobs, University of Florida; Paul Harvey, University of Colorado at Colorado Springs; Thomas J. Humphrey, Cleveland State University; and Ed Martini, Western Michigan University. Their thoughtful feedback was invaluable. I would also like to thank the seventy-eight student reviewers who offered commentary on the previous edition of this book.

At Bedford/St. Martin's, I would like to thank Chuck Christensen and Joan Feinberg, who conceived the original idea for this book. Special thanks go to Heidi Hood, Senior Editor at Bedford/St. Martin's, and my development editor Michelle McSweeney, whose careful reading, thoughtful analysis, and countless valuable suggestions have contributed so much to improving this edition. I would also like to thank Mary V. Dougherty, Publisher for History; Jane Knetzger, Director of Development for History; Lindsay DiGianvittorio, Production Editor; and copyeditor Janet Renard. In addition, I need to thank Susan Craig Murray, Director of Library and Learning Resources at the Winter Park Campus of Valencia Community College, for her excellent work on Appendix B of this manual. Finally, I am particularly grateful to my husband, Martin, and my very own college students, Geoff and Jonathan, who have patiently supported my work on this book through many years and six editions. As always, you're the best.

Mary Lynn Rampolla
Trinity Washington University
Washington, D.C.

(Continued from page iv)

Page 116: *A New Chart of the Atlantic or Western Ocean* (1797), Lawrence H. Slaughter Collection, The Lionel Pincus and Princess Firyal Map Division, The New York Public Library, Astor, Lenox and Tilden Foundations. Cover, *American Historical Review* vol. 112, no. 3 (June 2007). Published by the University of Chicago Press. © American Historical Association 2007. All rights reserved.

Page 116: Michael J. Sauter, "Clockwatchers and Stargazers: Time Discipline in Early Modern Berlin." *American Historical Review* vol. 112, no. 3 (June 2007): 685. Published by the University of Chicago Press. © American Historical Association 2007. All rights reserved.

Page 118: Reproduced by permission of University of Hawaii Press.

Page 127: Douglas O. Linder, Famous Trials Website, http://www.law .umkc.edu/faculty/projects/ftrials/salem/sal_acct.htm.

Page 127: Douglas O. Linder, Famous Trials Website, http://www.law .umkc.edu/faculty/projects/ftrials/ftrials.htm.

1

Introduction

WHY STUDY HISTORY?

As any Harry Potter fan knows, the most boring class at Hogwarts School of Witchcraft and Wizardry is History of Magic, taught by the dead (and "deadly dull") Professor Binns. The professor's droning lectures regularly send students into a stupefied trance, from which they emerge just long enough to scribble a few names or dates into their notes. Asked on one occasion about an unsolved mystery involving the school's past, Binns replies, "My subject is History of Magic. . . . I deal with facts, Miss Granger, not myths and legends."[1] Students who take their first college history class with a sense of foreboding often think that real historians, like Professor Binns, are interested only in compiling lists of names, dates, places, and "important" events that happened sometime in the past. But history is much more than this. The historian's goal is not to collect "facts" about the past, but rather to acquire insight into the ideas and realities that shaped the lives of men and women of earlier societies. Some beliefs and institutions of the past may seem alien to us; others are all too familiar. But in either case, when we study the people of the past, what we are really learning about is the rich diversity of human experience. The study of history is the study of the beliefs and desires, practices and institutions, of human beings.

Why should we bother studying the past in our increasingly future-oriented society? There are as many answers to that question as there are historians. First, a thoughtful examination of the past can tell us a great deal about how we came to be who we are. When we study history, we are looking at the roots of modern institutions, ideas, values, and problems. Second, the effort we put into grappling

---

1. J. K. Rowling, *Harry Potter and the Chamber of Secrets* (New York: Scholastic Press, 1999), 148–49.

with the worldviews of earlier societies teaches us to see the world through different eyes. The ability to recognize the meaning of events from a perspective other than our own is of inestimable value in our increasingly complex and multicultural society. Moreover, an awareness of various perspectives encourages students of history to engage in a critical analysis of their own culture and society and to recognize and critique their own assumptions. Finally, while historians, unlike Hogwarts' Professor Trelawney, don't have crystal balls with which to predict the future, an understanding of how past events have shaped the complex problems of our own times can help us make informed decisions about our future.

History is a complex discipline, and historians are a diverse group. They take different approaches to their material; they interpret events in different ways; they even disagree on such basic issues as whether and to what extent historians can be objective. These debates and disagreements amongst professional historians demonstrate the passion with which they approach their subject and ensure that the study of history will always remain fresh and exciting. Regardless of their approaches, however, all historians see writing as an important tool of inquiry and communication.

In addition to introducing you to some of the basic elements of what historians do, this manual provides guidelines for writing papers in the field of history at all levels, from first-year surveys to upper-division seminars. The vast majority of students enrolled in an undergraduate history course are not contemplating a career in history. Indeed, most history majors enter fields like law, government, business, and international relations. Nevertheless, the skills you will need to write an effective history paper—reading critically, thinking analytically, arguing persuasively, and writing clearly—will be useful to you wherever your academic interests take you and in whatever career path you choose to follow.

1a   Historical questions

Historians come to their work with a deep curiosity about the past; to satisfy that curiosity, they ask some of the same questions detectives ask: *Who? What? When? Where?* and *Why?* Some of those questions are designed to elicit "the facts" and are relatively easy to answer: *Who* was the emperor of Japan during World War II? *What* tools did eighteenth-century weavers use? *When* did the Vietnamese drive the Khmer Rouge out of Phnom Penh? *Where* was the first successful French settlement in Canada? Other questions, however, are less easy to answer: *Who* was Jack the Ripper? *What* were the religious beliefs of the peasants of twelfth-century Languedoc? *When* did President Nixon learn about the Watergate break-in? *Where* did the inhabitants of the original settlement at Roanoke go? *Why* did the civilization of the ancient Maya collapse? Complex questions such as these have formed the basis of absorbing historical studies.

Historians also need to analyze relationships between historical facts. Many of the questions historians ask, for example, reflect their interest in understanding the *context* in which events occurred. For instance, a historian interested in nineteenth-century science would not simply describe great "advances," such as Charles Darwin's publication of his theory of evolution by means of natural selection. As we know from the heated debates of our own time, science takes place within a social and cultural context, and scientific ideas can have a deep impact on politics, religion, education, and a host of other social institutions. Therefore, the historian would also consider questions about historical context: What role did political issues play in the acceptance or rejection of Darwin's theory? What other theories were current at the time, and how did they influence Darwin's thinking? Why did some theologians find his ideas threatening to religion, while others did not? What impact did larger social, political, and intellectual movements and institutions have on the study of biology in this period? In other words, historians do not examine events in isolation; rather, they try to understand the people and events of the past in terms of the unique historical context that helped shape them.

As they explore the relationships between and among events in the past, historians also examine the *causes* of events. The historical events that you will be studying and writing about can almost never be traced to a single cause, and historians are careful to avoid simplistic cause-and-effect relationships as explanations for events. For example, although the assassination of Archduke Franz Ferdinand is often cited as the event that precipitated World War I, no historian would argue that it *caused* the war. Rather, historians try to uncover the complex multiplicity of causes that grow out of the historical context in which events occurred.

Historians also ask questions about the relationship between *continuity* (events, conditions, ideas, and so on that remain the same over time) and *change*. Many of the questions historians ask reflect this interest. For example, a historian who asks, "What impact did the Black Death have on the economic and legal status of European peasants?" is interested in examining the changes brought about by the bubonic plague against the backdrop of the ongoing institution of serfdom.

Finally, while the past doesn't change, historians' interests—and the questions they ask—do. Historians, like the people they study, are part of a larger context. They are guided in their choice of subject and in their questions by their own interests and by the interests and concerns of their societies. As they ask new questions, historians look at sources in new ways. For example, in the 1950s, many standard U.S. history textbooks described Christopher Columbus as a heroic explorer; modern historians, writing from a more global perspective, have focused attention on the impact Columbus's explorations had on the indigenous peoples of the Americas. Historians may even discover "new" sources—sources that had always existed but had been ignored or dismissed as irrelevant. For example, the civil rights movement helped draw historians' attention to the central role of minorities in U.S. history.

History is a vital and dynamic discipline. We will never know all there is to know about the past because we are constantly posing new questions, and our questions, in turn, help us see the past in new ways. The best way to enter the world of the historian is to ask as many questions as you can about the particular historical issues you are studying. As you seek the answers, be aware of the new and more complex questions that your answers raise, and let those new questions guide your exploration further.

1b   How this manual can help you

When you do research and writing in a history course, you become a participant in historical debate. You devise questions about historical topics, seek answers to those questions in historical sources, and come to your own conclusions. In the papers you write, you need to construct arguments about the conclusions you have reached and offer support for them. This manual will help you understand the process from start to finish.

In Chapter 2, you will learn about the wide variety of sources historians use and how you can get the most out of them. Since critical reading is an integral part of effective writing in history, Chapter 3 walks you through some typical reading and short writing assignments given in history courses. Chapter 4 presents the nuts and bolts of writing an effective history essay, including how to develop a thesis, construct an argument, and organize your paper, while Chapter 5 is devoted entirely to how to write a research paper. Since all of the writing you do in history relies on your use of sources, Chapters 6 and 7 are designed to help you use your sources effectively while avoiding plagiarism. In addition, Chapter 7 includes models for documenting the sources you are most likely to use in an undergraduate history paper. Finally, Appendix A lists additional guides to writing in history, while Appendix B provides a list of resources you might wish to consult while doing research.

History, like other arts and sciences, provides a window onto the ideas and beliefs, the actions and passions, of human beings. Reading and writing history entail above all an exploration of who and what we are. This manual is designed to aid you in such exploration and to help you discover the pleasures of studying history.

2
Working with Sources

As you begin to think about historical questions, you will find that your search for answers will require you to explore a wide variety of sources. You will look at materials written in the period you are studying, and you will read books and articles written by modern historians. You may examine maps, photographs, paintings, and pottery. Ultimately, you may discover that you need to broaden your knowledge in a wide variety of areas, for history often takes its practitioners into all manner of related fields: literary criticism, art history, and archaeology; political science, economics, and sociology. In any case, you will need to learn how to work with the sources on which the study of history is based.

2a Identifying historical sources

To answer their questions, historians evaluate, organize, and interpret a wide variety of sources. These sources fall into two broad categories: primary sources and secondary sources. To study history and write history papers, you will need to know how to work with both kinds of sources.

2a-1 Primary sources

Primary sources are materials produced by people or groups directly involved in the event or topic under consideration, either as participants or as witnesses. They provide the evidence on which historians rely in order to describe and interpret the past. Some primary sources are written documents, such as letters; diaries; newspaper and magazine articles; speeches; autobiographies; treatises; census data; and marriage, birth, and death registers. In addition, historians often examine primary sources that are not written, like works of art, films, recordings, items of clothing, household objects, tools, and archaeological remains. For recent history, oral sources, such as interviews with Vietnam veterans or Holocaust survivors and other such eyewitness accounts, can also be primary sources. By examining primary sources, historians gain insights into the thoughts, behaviors, and experiences of the people of the past.

Sometimes, you may be able to work directly with primary source materials, such as letters or manuscripts in an archive. More often, you will use print or electronic versions of sources, such as edited and/or translated collections of letters or documents, images of maps or paintings, or facsimiles. (For more on evaluating edited and translated sources, see p. 11.) In either case, primary sources provide windows into the past that allow you to develop your own interpretation, rather than rely on the interpretation of another historian.

2a-2 Secondary sources

Historians also use *secondary sources*: books and articles in scholarly journals that comment on and interpret primary sources. Secondary sources are extremely useful. Reading secondary sources is often the simplest and quickest way to become acquainted with what is already known about the subject you are studying. In addition, examining scholarly books and articles will inform you about the ways in which other historians have understood and interpreted events. Reading a variety of secondary sources is also the best way to become aware of the issues and interpretations that are the subject of controversy and debate among professional historians, debates in which you, as a student of history, are invited to participate. In addition, the bibliographies of secondary sources can direct you to primary sources and additional secondary sources that you might find useful.

As valuable as secondary sources are, you should never base a history paper on them alone, unless, of course, you are writing a historiography paper (see 3b-6). Whenever possible, you should work from primary sources, studying the events of the past in the words of people who experienced, witnessed, or participated in them.

2a-3 Primary or secondary? The changing status of a source

While the definitions provided above seem fairly straight-forward, it is not always easy to determine whether a particular text is a primary source or a secondary source. This is because the status of a source as primary or secondary does not depend on how old the source is, but rather on the historical question you are asking. For example, if you are writing about the reign of Julius Caesar (100–44 BCE), Suetonius's *Lives of the Twelve Caesars*, written in the early second century CE, would be a *secondary* source because Suetonius was not a witness to the events he describes. If, however, you are writing about the debates among second-century Romans about the use and abuse of imperial power, Suetonius's work would be a *primary* source. Thus, the status of a source as primary or secondary depends on the focus of your research.

Note: How you access a source does not affect its status as a primary or secondary source. You can find both primary sources (such as collections of letters, newspapers, and photographs) and secondary sources (such as journal articles and books) in your library; you can also find both online. For example, *The Complete Work of Charles Darwin Online*, published by Cambridge University (http://darwin-online.org.uk), includes facsimiles of Darwin's notebooks, letters, and other original documents that would be considered primary sources. Similarly, many scholarly articles, which originally appeared in print journals, can also be accessed through electronic databases or archives such as *JSTOR*. (For more information about electronic databases, see 5c-4 and Appendix B.) Whether you access such articles in print or online, these are secondary sources.

2a-4 Uses of primary and secondary sources

Both primary and secondary sources can provide valuable information; however, they provide different kinds of information. Primary sources allow you to enter the lives and minds of the people you are studying. The documents people wrote—sermons and wills, novels and poems—and the things they made—music and movies, knife blades and buttons—bring you into direct contact with the world of the past. Secondary sources, in contrast, are written by historians who can provide a broader perspective on the events of the past than the people who actually participated in them since they have more information about the context and outcome of those events, an awareness of multiple points of view, and access to more documents than any single participant. In studying nineteenth-century communes, for example, primary sources such as diaries, letters, or items that commune members produced and used can provide firsthand information about the thoughts, feelings, and daily lives of the people who lived in such communities. Primary sources would be less useful, however, in examining the larger sociological effects of communal living. To get a better understanding of those effects, secondary sources in which historians examine several such communities over time, or study the ways in which contemporary outsiders viewed communes, might prove more useful. In your own work, you will need to use both primary and secondary sources, always keeping in mind what kinds of information each of those sources can tell you about a topic.

2b Evaluating sources

If primary sources always told the truth, the historian's job would be much easier—and also rather boring. But sources, like witnesses in a murder case, often lie. Sometimes they lie on purpose, telling untruths to further a specific ideological, philosophical, personal, or political agenda. Sometimes they lie by omission, leaving out bits of information that are crucial to interpreting an event. Sometimes sources mislead unintentionally because the author's facts were incomplete, incorrect, or misinterpreted. Many sources are biased, either consciously or unconsciously, and contain unstated assumptions; all reflect the interests and concerns of their authors. Moreover, primary sources often conflict. As a result, one of the challenges historians face in writing a history paper is evaluating the reliability and usefulness of their sources.

Like primary sources, secondary sources may contradict one another. Several historians can examine the same set of materials and interpret them in very different ways. Similarly, historians can try to answer the same questions by looking at different kinds of evidence or by using different methods to gather, evaluate, and interpret evidence. To get the most out of your reading of secondary sources, you will need to study a variety of interpretations of historical events and issues.

You can find general advice about critical reading in Chapter 3 (see pp. 20–23); the following sections provide specific suggestions for evaluating both primary and secondary sources.

2b-1 Evaluating primary sources

Since primary sources originate in the actual period under discussion, we might be inclined to trust what they say implicitly. After all, if the author is an eyewitness, why should anyone doubt his or her word? Alternatively, we might lean toward dismissing primary sources altogether on the grounds that they are too subjective; as any police investigator could tell you, eyewitnesses see different things and remember them in different ways. In fact, historians steer a middle ground between these two approaches. Although primary sources comprise the basic material with which they work, historians do not take the evidence provided by such sources simply at face value. Like good detectives, they evaluate the evidence, approaching their sources analytically and critically.

Historians have developed a variety of techniques for evaluating primary sources. One such technique is to compare sources; a fact or description contained in one source is more likely to be accepted as trustworthy if other sources support or corroborate it. Another technique is to identify the author's biases. For example, the historian Polydore Vergil asserted in his book *Anglica Historia* that King Richard III killed his nephews. Since Vergil was a contemporary of Richard III, you might accept his account at face value, unless you were also aware that the book was commissioned by King Henry VII, an enemy of Richard III who had organized a rebellion against him, killed him in battle, and seized his throne. Taking this fact into consideration, you would want to approach Vergil's work with a more critical eye, considering whether his loyalty to his employer led to any bias in his history. Historians also read their sources carefully for evidence of internal contradictions or logical inconsistencies, and they pay attention to their sources' use of language, since the adjectives and metaphors an author uses can point to hidden biases and unspoken assumptions.

Tips for Writers
Questions for Evaluating Text-Based Primary Sources

- Who is the author?
- When was the source composed?
- Who was the intended audience?
- What is the purpose of the source? (Note that some primary sources, such as letters to the editor, have a central theme or argument and are intended to persuade; others, such as census data, are purely factual.)
- How do the author's gender and socioeconomic class compare to those of the people about whom he or she is writing?
- What is the historical context in which the source was written and read?
- What unspoken assumptions does the text contain?
- What biases are detectable in the source?
- Was the original text commissioned by anyone or published by a press with a particular viewpoint?
- How do other contemporary sources compare with this one?

Special considerations for editions and translations

- Is the source complete? If not, does the text contain an introductory note explaining editorial decisions?
- If you are using a document in a collection, does the editor explain his or her process of selection and/or translation?
- Are there notes introducing individual documents that provide useful information about the text?
- Are there footnotes or endnotes that alert you to alternate readings or translations of the material in the text?
- Are you using an edition or translation that most accurately reflects the current state of scholarship?

Thinking about editions and translations. As an undergraduate, you will probably not have the opportunity that professional historians do to work with original documents in their original languages. Instead, you will likely be relying on published, translated editions of primary sources or, increasingly, on documents posted on the Internet.

Using modern editions of sources in translation is an excellent way to enter into the worldview of the people you are studying. Be aware, however, that any edited text reflects, to some extent, the interests and experiences of the editor or translator. For example, the process by which

Tips for Writers

Questions for Evaluating Nonwritten Primary Sources

For artifacts

- When and where was the artifact made?
- Who might have used it, and what might it have been used for?
- What does the artifact tell us about the people who made and used it and the period in which it was made?

For art works (paintings, sculpture, etc.)

- Who is the artist and how does the work compare to his or her other works?
- When and why was the work made? Was it commissioned? If so, by whom?
- Was the work part of a larger artistic or intellectual movement?
- Where was the work first displayed? How did contemporaries respond to it? How do their responses compare to the ways in which it is understood now?

For photographs

- Who is the photographer? Why did he or she take this photograph?
- Where was the photograph first published or displayed? Did that publication or venue have a particular mission or point of view?
- Are there any obvious details such as angle, contrast, or cropping that suggest bias?

For cartoons

- What is the message of the cartoon? How do words and images combine to convey that message?
- In what kind of publication did it originally appear (newspaper, magazine, etc.)? Did that publication have a particular agenda or mission?
- When did the cartoon appear? How might its historical context be significant?

For maps

- What kind of map is this (topographical, political, military, etc.)?
- Where and when was the map made? What was its intended purpose?
- Does the map contain any extraneous text or images? If so, what do they add to our understanding of the map itself?

For sound recordings

- Who made the recording and what kind of recording is it (music, speech, interview, etc.)?
- Was the recording originally intended for broadcast? If so, why was it broadcast and who was the intended audience?

For video and film

- What kind of film is this (documentary, feature, etc.)?
- Who is the director, producer, and screenwriter for the film? Have they made other films to which you can compare this one?
- Who is the intended audience? Why was the film made?
- Does the film use particular cinematic techniques that convey a particular mood or tone? (For more on analyzing film, see 3b-4.)

the editor of a document collection selects which documents to include and which to leave out involves interpretation: the collection, as it appears in print, reflects how the editor has understood and organized the material and what he or she sees as significant. Similarly, excerpts from long documents can be useful in introducing you to the basic content and flavor of a document, but it is important to note that in the process of choosing excerpts, the editor of a document is making a judgment about what aspects of the source are important. You should read the whole source, if possible, rather than excerpts, in order to understand the significance of the entire document and the context of any portions of the source that you wish to discuss or quote. Finally, translation always involves decisions about word choice and grammar that can range from inconsequential to very significant.

Note: Often, the introduction to an edited volume, or the short headnotes that introduce individual texts in a collection, will not only provide useful background information about the text but also alert you to the editor's choices and intentions.

Primary documents require both careful and critical reading in order to be effective research sources. When you analyze a primary source, keep in mind the questions in the Tips for Writers box on page 11.

Thinking about nonwritten primary sources. Although historians work mainly from written sources, they also use a wide variety of nonwritten materials, including works of art, photographs, maps, and audio and video recordings. When dealing with nonwritten primary sources, you should consider the same questions about author, audience, and context that are outlined in the Tips for Writers box on page 11, while adding some questions from the Tips for Writers box on pages 12–13 that are specific to the type of source you are considering.

Evaluating primary sources: an example. In a letter written to Sheik El-Messiri in 1798, Napoleon expresses the hope that the sheik will soon establish a government in Egypt based on the principles of the Qur'an, the sacred text of Islam. Those principles, according to Napoleon, "alone are true and capable of bringing happiness to men."[1] Should we assume, on the evidence of this letter, that Napoleon believed in the truth of Islam? A historian might ask, "Do we have any other evidence for Napoleon's attitude toward Islam? What do other primary sources tell us about Napoleon's attitude toward religions such as Catholicism, Protestantism, and Judaism? Do any other primary sources contradict the attitude toward Islam expressed in Napoleon's letter to the sheik?" In other words, "How accurately and to what extent can this source answer questions about Napoleon's religious beliefs?" In addition, historians try to understand or interpret their sources even if those sources do not offer the best or most accurate information on a certain topic. As it happens, Napoleon did not believe in Islam. This does not mean, however, that his letter to the sheik has no value. Instead, a good historian will ask, "Under what circumstances did Napoleon write this letter? Who was Sheik El-Messiri, and what was his relationship to Napoleon? What does this letter tell us about Napoleon's willingness to use religion to his political advantage?" Thus, to write about historical questions, you will need to know how to approach many different kinds of primary sources and ask appropriate questions of them. (For more on writing about primary sources, see Chapters 3 and 4.)

---

1. Napoleon Bonaparte, "Letter to the Sheik El-Messiri," in *The Mind of Napoleon: Selection from His Written and Spoken Words*, 4th ed., trans. and ed. J. Christopher Herold (New York: Columbia University Press, 1969), 104.

2b-2 Evaluating secondary sources

Reading secondary sources helps us understand how other historians have interpreted the primary sources for the period being studied. Students sometimes hesitate to question the conclusions of established scholars; nevertheless, as with primary sources, it is important to read secondary sources critically and analytically, asking the same questions you ask of primary sources. Evaluate a secondary source by asking the critical questions listed in the Tips for Writers box on page 16. (For more on critical reading, see 3a.) In addition to the critical questions listed in that box, it is especially important to do the following when you work with a secondary source:

Consider the implications of the publication date. If it is important that you know the most recent theories about a historical subject, pay special attention to the publication dates of the sources you are considering. A 2000 article reviewing theories about the construction of Native American burial mounds may contain more recent ideas than a 1964 review. Do not assume, however, that newer interpretations are always better; some older works have contributed significantly to the field and may offer interpretations that are still influential. (As you become more experienced in historical research, you will be able to determine which older sources are still useful.) Moreover, older sources might offer a historical perspective on how interpretations of an issue or event have changed over time, which is particularly important if you are writing a historiographic essay (see 3b-6).

Evaluate the logic of the author's argument. Any book or article makes an argument in support of a thesis. (For detailed information on what a thesis is, see 4c; for a discussion of how the thesis relates to the argument of a paper, see 4d.) Once you have identified the author's thesis, you should evaluate the evidence he or she uses to support it. You may not be in a position to judge the accuracy of the evidence, although you will build expertise as you continue to read about the subject. You can, however, evaluate the way in which the author uses the evidence he or she presents. You might ask yourself whether the evidence logically supports the author's point. For example, Margaret Sanger, who founded the American Birth Control League in 1921, was also involved in the U.S. eugenics movement, which advocated, among other things, for the sterilization of individuals deemed "mentally incompetent." This, however, does not justify the conclusion that *all* early-twentieth-century birth control advocates favored eugenics. Such an assertion would be a logical fallacy known as a *hasty generalization*.

You should also ask whether the same facts could be interpreted in another way to support a different thesis. For example, G. Stanley Hall, an early-twentieth-century American psychologist, amassed evidence that demonstrated a correlation between a woman's educational level and the number of children she had: Women who attended colleges and universities had fewer children than their less educated sisters. From this fact, he concluded that higher education caused sterility in women.

Tips for Writers
Questions for Evaluating Secondary Sources

- Who is the author? What are his or her academic credentials? (You will often find information about the author in the preface of a book; journals sometimes include authors' biographies, either on the first page of the article or in a separate section.)
- When was the text written? (On the importance of publication dates, see p. 15.)
- Who is the publisher? Is the text published by a scholarly press or a popular one? (For more information on scholarly and popular presses, see p. 17.)
- Who is the intended audience for the text (scholars, students, general reading public, etc.)?
- What is the author's main argument or thesis? (For more on identifying the author's thesis, see p. 22.)
- Does the author use primary sources as evidence to support his or her thesis? Is the author's interpretation of the primary sources persuasive?
- Is there primary source evidence that you are aware of that the author does not consider?
- Does the author contradict or disagree with others who have written on the subject? If so, does he or she acknowledge and effectively address opposing arguments or interpretations?
- Do the footnotes/endnotes and bibliography reference other important works on the same topic?
- Does the author build his or her argument on any unsubstantiated assumptions? (See pp. 15–17.)

A modern historian looking at the same evidence might conclude that education allowed women to become economically independent, freed them from the necessity of forming early marriages, and allowed them to pursue careers other than raising children.

Another consideration is whether the cause-and-effect relationships described in a source are legitimate. It may be true that event A happened before event B, but that does not necessarily mean that A caused B. For example, on July 20, 1969, Neil Armstrong became the first person to walk on the moon. The following winter was particularly harsh in the United States. We should not conclude, however, that the lunar landing caused a change in weather patterns. This would be a *post hoc* fallacy, from the Latin *post hoc, ergo propter hoc* (after this, therefore because of this).

Finally, consider how the author deals with any counterevidence. (See 4d-2 for a discussion of counterevidence.)

Distinguish between popular and scholarly sources. If you consult secondary sources for your paper, it is important that you use scholarly, rather than popular, sources. Scholarly sources are written by experts in the field; usually, they are peer-reviewed—evaluated by other scholars—before being published. To determine whether a secondary source is scholarly or popular, consider the following questions:

- Does the author have academic credentials?
- Does the book or article have notes, a bibliography, and other academic apparatus?
- Is the source published by an academic press?
- Does the book or article analyze and interpret primary sources or the work of other scholars?

If you are still not sure whether a book or article you want to use is an appropriate secondary source, consult your professor or a reference librarian.

Note: While popular magazines are not appropriate *secondary* sources, they can be excellent *primary* sources for certain research topics. You might, for example, consult back issues of *Time* magazine in order to explore how the news media covered the collapse of the Soviet Union, or examine the advertisements in *Good Housekeeping* for a paper on women's economic importance in the period between the two world wars.

2b-3 Evaluating online sources

As noted above, the Internet provides ready access to both primary and secondary sources. Editions of a wide variety of written primary sources (letters, treatises, government publications, even whole books) are available on the Internet, as are cartoons, photographs, images of antique maps, and other nonwritten primary sources. (For a list of some databases containing primary sources of interest to historians, see Appendix B.) If you are looking for secondary sources, historians may publish their research online in electronic journals like the *E-Journal of Portuguese History* (http://www.brown.edu/Departments/ Portuguese_Brazilian_Studies/ejph/); in addition, digitized versions of countless scholarly articles are available in electronic databases such as *JSTOR: The Scholarly Journal Archive* (http://www.jstor.org/), which scans and archives a wide variety of scholarly print journals. (For a list of useful electronic sources, see Appendix B.)

Web sites maintained by universities, museums, government agencies, and other institutions can be a gold mine for students whose access to large research libraries is limited. Making effective use of the Internet as a research tool, however, requires you to anticipate and avoid the special problems that it presents.

The most significant difficulty you may encounter when trying to evaluate a source accessed online is determining its credibility. When working with such a source, first determine if it has a print or real-life equivalent. Is it an article from a journal that is published in print? Is it an artifact that resides in a museum? If the source actually exists in physical form, you can refer to the Tips for Writers box on pages 12–13 to help you study and evaluate it. If, however, the source exists only online, you must use extra caution in evaluating it. This is because, while articles in scholarly journals and books from academic presses are carefully reviewed by other scholars in the field, anyone with Internet access can create a Web site or a blog. You should also be aware that many popular online resources are not appropriate sources for scholarly research. For example, *Wikipedia*, the widely used online encyclopedia, is comprised of entries written largely by anonymous authors. The entries are not peer-reviewed; moreover, anyone can modify a *Wikipedia* entry. Therefore, even though many of its entries may be informative and accurate, *Wikipedia* cannot be considered a reliable academic source.

The questions in the Tips for Writers box below will help you determine whether an online source is reliable. In general, the most worthwhile sites with the most accurate sources will probably have a scholarly affiliation. You can find reputable sites by consulting your professor or a reference librarian, or by browsing Appendix B.

Tips for Writers
Questions for Evaluating Online Sources

- Is the author's identity clear? If so, what are his or her academic credentials? Does the author list an academic degree? Is he or she affiliated with a college or university? Are there other Web sites that provide additional information about the author?

- Does the author provide evidence for his or her assertions, such as citations and bibliographies? Are the sources up to date? Are the sources for statistics included?

- Is the site affiliated with an academic institution, press, or journal? The Web address—or URL—can provide some clues to such affiliations. If *.edu* or *.gov* appears in the address, it has been posted by an educational or governmental institution, which should give you a greater degree of confidence in the material it contains.

- Is the site sponsored by a particular organization? (Look for *.org* in the URL.) Do you know anything about the interests and concerns of the person or group that publishes the site? (Check the home page or click on "About" to find a mission statement.) Does the organization seem biased?

- Does the site allow users to add or change content? If so, the site cannot be relied on to provide accurate information, even if it includes notes, references to academic sources, or useful links. (This is the case, for example, with *Wikipedia* articles, which often include scholarly apparatus but can be altered by any user.)

- What is the purpose of the site? Is it designed to inform? Persuade? Sell a product?

- Does the information on the site coincide with what you have learned about the subject from other sources?

- Has the site been updated recently?

- Does the site contain useful links to other sites? Are the linked sites affiliated with reputable institutions or persons? If you are still unsure if an online source is reliable, it is best to consult your professor or a reference librarian.

3

Reading and Writing in History

SOME TYPICAL ASSIGNMENTS

Most scholars would agree that reading and writing are interrelated processes. As you read, you begin to see new connections between the ideas, people, and events you are studying. Then, as you begin to write, new questions arise, prompting you to look at the texts you have already read in new ways and find new materials that might help you answer your questions. This chapter introduces you to the process of reading actively and discusses some typical writing assignments that measure your ability to read accurately, critically, and analytically.

3a Reading actively in history

History courses typically require a great deal of reading from a wide variety of sources; even nonwritten sources need to be critically analyzed or "read." Consequently, reading is the assignment you will encounter most frequently. If your professor has assigned a textbook, you will probably be expected to read a chapter or two each week. In addition, you may be asked to read a variety of secondary sources, including articles from scholarly journals or books about a particular aspect of your subject. Many professors also assign primary sources, documents ranging from medieval chronicles to legal documents to newspaper accounts. (For a fuller discussion of primary and secondary sources, including advice for evaluating nonwritten sources, see Chapter 2.) If you are writing a research paper, you will need to find, read, and analyze a variety of sources pertaining to your topic that are not part of the reading assigned to the whole class. Since reading is such an important assignment, it is essential to give serious consideration to how you read.

Reading for a history course is not like reading a best-selling novel for personal enjoyment; it is not enough to skim each page once and get the gist of the story. Similarly, you should avoid the common, but not very useful, habit of reading passively, plodding through a text line by line in hopes of absorbing some of the material it contains. To do your best work in history, you will need to become an active reader. In contrast to passive readers, active readers are engaged in a dialogue with the text. They ask questions, make comments, and connect what they are reading to information they already know and texts they have already read. This kind of careful and critical reading is crucial both for active and intelligent participation in class discussion and for writing effective papers.

As you read in history, you must accomplish several tasks. Obviously, you need to understand the content, but you must also *evaluate* its usefulness, *analyze* its significance, and *synthesize* all of your reading into one coherent picture of the topic you are studying. Evaluating sources was the subject of Chapter 2; Chapters 4 and 5 will address the process of synthesis. This chapter suggests some reading strategies that will help you analyze or think critically about a source.

Pre-read the text. Before you even begin to read, you should try to get a sense of the scope of the book or article and what it might tell you. If you are reading a book, note its subtitle, if any; examine the table of contents; check for appendices and lists of maps and/or illustrations. If you are reading an article, look for an abstract at the beginning of the text and check for section headings. If you are examining a primary source, read the introduction to the text or the headnote to the document. For both books and articles, look at the bibliography and determine how extensive any footnotes or endnotes are. Spending a few minutes on such pre-reading tasks will help you determine how to approach your reading and consequently make it more productive.

Determine the author's thesis. Passive readers read as if everything a book or article contains is equally important; following the advice of the King of Hearts in *Alice in Wonderland*, they "begin at the beginning, go on . . . to the end, then stop," picking up bits of information somewhat haphazardly as they go. Active readers begin by identifying the text's thesis—the conclusion that the author has reached as a result of his or her research and analysis. Since the argument of a book or article is designed to demonstrate the thesis, understanding a source's main idea enables readers to absorb the text more effectively. (For additional information, see 4c.) The quickest way to identify an author's thesis is to read the preface, introduction, and conclusion of a book, or the first few paragraphs of an article. It is usually in these sections that an author states his or her main points. (Looking at the last chapter of a history book is not cheating, nor will it spoil the ending, unless you have been assigned a historical mystery, like Josephine Tey's excellent novel *The Daughter of Time*.)

Read with the author's thesis in mind. If you are reading a book or article about a subject that is new to you, it is tempting to get caught up in the details and try to remember all of the facts. However, because the historian's goal is not simply to *collect* facts but to *organize* and *interpret* them in a way that allows us to better understand the people and societies of the past, it is much more useful to read a book or article with an eye to understanding how an author builds an argument in support of his or her interpretation, or thesis. In order to do this, you should identify the main pieces of evidence the author cites in support of his or her conclusions. Often, the first sentence (or topic sentence) of the body paragraphs in an article or the introductory paragraphs of each chapter of a book will indicate the most important elements of an author's argument. (For more information, see 4d and 4e.)

Ask questions of the text. As you read with the author's thesis in mind, you should constantly interrogate the text: What is the author's point here? Why has he or she chosen this example? Do you disagree with any points the author makes, and if so, why? As you try to answer these rather broad and general questions, new, more tightly focused and nuanced questions will arise, taking you deeper into the text. In this way, asking questions of the text helps you read with increasing sophistication and insight.

Write as you read. Active readers are *physically* active, writing as they read. Writing while reading serves several functions. Writing directly in the margins of the text (provided, of course, that the text belongs to you) can help you locate important or confusing passages that you want to return to later. In addition, taking notes in your own words can help you remember what you have read and help you solidify your understanding of the text. Finally, writing as you read will help you clarify your thoughts about what you are reading and provide direction for further reading and research.

The writing you do while reading can take many different forms; some useful suggestions appear in the Tips for Writers box below.

Review what you have written. While writing itself helps many people remember what they have read, it is particularly useful to review your notes periodically. Make sure you have answered the questions that the reading raised for you and compared the arguments of each text you are reading with the other readings for the class.

Tips for Writers
Writing as You Read

- Underline or highlight important points, including the thesis and topic sentences.
- Look up unfamiliar words in a dictionary and write their definitions in the margins of the text.
- Talk back to the text by writing notations in the margins. Include questions you want to answer, disagreements you have with the author's argument, and cross-references to other materials you have read on the subject.
- Write summaries of your reading to ensure that you have understood the material. (See 3b-1 for advice on summaries.)
- Copy out, in quotation marks, any particularly striking phrases or statements that you might want to quote directly in your work, and note complete bibliographic information. (See 5d for further advice on effective note taking.)
- Keep a journal in which you can record any ideas, insights, or questions that occur to you as you read.

3b Writing about reading

When students imagine the writing assignments they might receive in a history class, they usually think about short essays and research papers, which will be discussed in detail in Chapters 4 and 5. However, history students are frequently given writing assignments with which they may be less familiar: summaries, annotated bibliographies, critiques of books or journal articles, analyses of individual primary sources, and historiographic essays. Each is based on a close, critical reading of one or more texts, but each requires a slightly different approach.

Note: Since the specifics of your assignment may vary from the examples below, you should always read your assignment carefully and consult your professor if you have questions.

3b-1 Summaries

History students are often required to read complex and difficult texts. As a result, many professors find it useful for students to write a summary, or *précis*, of a particularly challenging or complicated document, article, or section of a book.

Writing a summary requires you to condense what you have read and describe the author's central ideas in your own words; it helps ensure that you have understood and digested the material. A summary should not include your reaction to or critical analysis of the text. Rather, a summary should recount the author's main point, or thesis, and the key evidence (examples, illustrations, statistics, and so on) used to support it. You should note that you will not be able to include *all* of the author's evidence; identifying the *most important* evidence is part of the challenge of writing a summary.

In writing your summary, it is essential that the wording and turns of phrase be entirely your own and not those of the text you are summarizing. To do otherwise is plagiarism, which is no more acceptable in a summary than in any other kind of writing. (For a detailed discussion of plagiarism and how to avoid it, see Chapter 6.)

3b-2 Annotated bibliographies

When you start to study an unfamiliar topic or begin to work on a research paper, you will need to identify and evaluate the materials that will enable you to develop an understanding of the general topic and what other scholars have said about it, and form your own interpretations of the sources. In other words, you will need to generate a bibliography.

A *bibliography* is a list of books and articles on a specific topic; it may include both primary and secondary sources. An *annotated bibliography* begins with the information included in a bibliography and then expands on it by including a brief summary of each book or article and assessing its value for the topic under discussion. An annotated bibliography, then, demonstrates your ability to gather, examine, and evaluate materials pertaining to a particular subject.

An annotated bibliography is an especially versatile and flexible assignment, so you should pay careful attention to the instructions provided by your professor. Regardless of the length or scope of the assignment, however, entries in an annotated bibliography generally follow a similar format. The entries should be arranged alphabetically by authors' last names. (See 7c-2 for complete information about how to write bibliographic entries for a variety of sources.) Following the bibliographic information, you should include an *annotation*—a short paragraph in which you describe the content of the book and its usefulness for your topic. The following are some elements you might include in an annotation:

- A one-sentence description of what the book is about, including the author's thesis.
- A brief description of who the author is and what his or her credentials are.
- A brief description of the evidence the author uses to support his or her thesis.
- A concise evaluation of the author's use of sources and the validity of his or her argument.
- A brief description of the value of the book for your project.

Remember that entries in an annotated bibliography should be relatively short; you will not be able to write a full analysis of a book or article, as you would in a book review or critique (see 3b-3). Nevertheless, you will be able to indicate the overall content of the source and its value for your project.

The following is a sample annotated bibliography entry:

Fletcher, Richard. *The Cross and the Crescent: Christianity and Islam from Muhammad to the Reformation*. New York: Penguin/Viking, 2004.

> This book examines the interactions, both positive and negative, between Christianity and Islam in the medieval and early modern periods. Fletcher, formerly a professor of medieval history at the University of York, England, argues that despite some productive interactions in the areas of trade and intellectual life, Christians and Muslims did not achieve any real measure of mutual understanding in the period under discussion. Rather, relations between the two cultures were marked by fear and hostility on the Christian side, and disdain and aloofness on the part of Muslims. Fletcher cites numerous examples to demonstrate that even in the most multicultural parts of the medieval world (Spain, Sicily, the Latin crusader states), Christians and Muslims "lived side by side, but did not blend" (p. 116). Although Fletcher's book is brief (161 pages), it is both scholarly and eminently readable, even for a non-specialist, and provides a clearly argued introduction to the subject that elucidates both Muslim and Christian viewpoints. Footnotes enable the student to pursue the sources the author used, and a narrative bibliography provides suggestions for further reading. The book also includes a useful chronology.

3b-3 Critiques and book reviews

In order to demonstrate your ability to read a text critically and analytically, you may be asked to critique an article or review a book (a book review is simply a critique of a full-length book). You may feel unqualified to complete such an assignment; after all, the author of the text is a professional historian. However, even if you cannot write from the same level of experience and knowledge as the author, you can write an effective review if you understand what the assignment requires. Reviews and critiques of texts begin with careful, active, and critical reading. (See 3a for advice on reading critically.) Active reading requires you to keep the author's thesis in mind, note the evidence used to support that thesis, ask the critical questions for evaluating sources outlined in Chapter 2, and note your reactions and responses to the text as you go. Your review or critique then grows out of this active reading.

A review or critique is not the same thing as a book report, which simply summarizes the content of a book. Nor does a review or critique merely report your reaction (for example, "This book was boring" or "I liked this article"). Rather, when writing a review or critique, you not only report on the content of the text and your response to it but also assess its strengths and weaknesses. So, for example, it is not enough to say "This book is not very good"; you need to explain and/or justify your reaction through an analysis of the text. Did you find the book unconvincing because the author did not supply enough evidence to support his or her assertions? Is the logic faulty? Or did you disagree with the book's underlying assumptions? Finally, note that *critical* does not mean "negative." If a book is well written and presents an original thesis supported by convincing evidence, say so. A good book review does not have to be negative; it does have to be fair and analytical. (Incidentally, when you are writing your critique or review, it is unnecessary to preface statements with *I think* or *in my opinion* since readers assume that as a reviewer you are expressing your own opinions.)

Though there is no one correct way to structure a critique or review, the following is a possible approach:

- Summarize the book or article, and relate the author's main point, or thesis. Make sure you briefly identify the author and note his or her credentials.
- Describe the author's viewpoint and purpose for writing; note any aspects of the author's background that are important for understanding the text.
- Note the most important evidence the author presents to support his or her thesis.
- Evaluate the author's use of evidence and describe how he or she deals with counterevidence. (See 4d-2 for a discussion of counterevidence.) Is the argument convincing?
- Compare this text with other books or articles you have read on the same subject.
- Conclude with a final evaluation of the book or article. You might discuss who would find it useful and why.

Note: While many of the elements of a review or critique are the same as those found in an annotated bibliography entry, full-length book reviews and article critiques should be much longer and more detailed than brief bibliography entries.

3b-4 Film reviews

You may be surprised to find a discussion of film reviews in a chapter called "Reading and Writing in History." However, a discussion of film in this context is appropriate for two reasons. First, while historians primarily rely on written texts, film and other visual texts have become increasingly important historical sources. Second, watching a film, like reading a book, should not be a passive exercise. If you use film as a historical source, you will need to approach or "read" a film with the same critical and analytical skills that you would apply to a written text. Just as there are different kinds of written texts, so too are there different kinds of films. The most common types of films historians use are documentaries and feature films. Identifying which type of film you are dealing with is the essential first step in writing a film review.

Documentaries

Documentaries are films that use primary sources (such as photographs, paintings, and documents) and commentaries on those sources by various authorities (such as historians, biographers, and eyewitnesses) to construct a narrative of a historical figure or event. For this reason, documentaries should be considered secondary sources. Ken Burns's series *The Civil War*, which uses primary sources such as documents and photographs as well as commentary from historians, is a good example of this type of film.

Documentaries about events of the twentieth and twenty-first centuries are able to make use of a unique primary source: *footage*. Footage is a direct film or videotape recording of an event. Footage can be produced by professionals, such as television news videographers, or by amateurs, like Abraham Zapruder's 8mm film of the assassination of John F. Kennedy. Footage is a primary source since it records events as they happen.

A documentary filmmaker's use of primary sources such as footage must be viewed critically. Filmmakers, like writers, choose what to record. Sometimes luck plays a part in the images they capture; filmmaker Jules Naudet was working on a documentary about the New York City Firefighting Academy when he filmed the hijacked plane hitting Tower 1 of the World Trade Center on September 11, 2001. Usually, however, they are filming with a particular purpose, and sometimes with a particular audience in mind. Moreover, footage that makes its way to a news broadcast has been cut and edited. In evaluating a documentary that uses footage, it is useful to know why and by whom the original footage was shot and whether and for what purposes it has been edited.

Feature films

Feature films are films designed primarily as entertainment. They sometimes feature famous actors and always aim at box-office success. Historical rigor is not usually their primary concern, so we should not be surprised to find that such films vary dramatically in the accuracy with which they depict the period, events, and historical figures they ostensibly portray. At one end of the spectrum are films like *The Return of Martin Guerre*, which is based on a true story about a peasant who abandoned his family and the impostor who successfully took his place. The director, Daniel Vigne, consulted historical documents, attempted faithfully to re-create the material culture of the period, and made extensive use of historian Natalie Zemon Davis as a consultant. Consequently, this film might be considered a secondary source for our understanding of French peasant life in seventeenth-century France. In contrast, in his 1916 film *Joan the Woman*, legendary director Cecil B. DeMille took serious liberties with the historical accounts of Joan of Arc, inventing a love interest for her and linking her story with the English efforts against the Germans in France during World War I. DeMille's film has virtually no value as a secondary source for the history of Joan of Arc, but it is a valuable primary source for understanding American attitudes toward the Great War and the role of filmmakers in encouraging the United States to join the conflict. This points to an important consideration: *all* feature films can be viewed as primary sources for the cultural and social history of the period in which they were made.

Because of the growing importance of film of all sorts, writing a film review is an increasingly common assignment. The suggestions provided in 3b-3 for writing a critique or book review also apply to a film review. In addition, you should do the following:

- Determine whether the film is a documentary or a feature film. Who is the intended audience, and for what reason was the film made?

- If the film is a documentary, note the academic credentials of the experts who provide the commentary. If it is a feature film, determine whether the filmmaker made use of professional historians as consultants.

- For documentaries and feature films, analyze the interests and concerns of the producer, director, and screenwriter. Note any other films they have produced, directed, or written that might help the viewer understand their interests and biases. In this context, it is useful to determine whether the people most responsible for the film have provided interviews or written commentary that might shed light on their work.

- Think about how the visual images presented in the film enhance our understanding of the subject and the period. Do the costumes and sets accurately portray the historical reality of the period? Does the film help us understand the material culture of the period?

- Analyze the cinematic techniques used to convey the story. Is the film shot in black-and-white or in color? How does the filmmaker use lighting to convey a mood or to make a symbolic point? How is one set of images juxtaposed with another to create an impression? What kinds of camera angles are used, and why?

- Analyze how the filmmaker uses sound. What kind of music is used in the soundtrack? Was it composed specifically for the film, or are classical or popular pieces used?

- Discuss the ways in which the filmmaker shapes the narrative. From what point of view is the story told? Does the film employ flashbacks or narrative voice-overs?

- If the film is based on a play or a specific text, compare the film with the original source. Are there any themes or concepts portrayed more effectively in the film than in the text? Conversely, are there elements of the source that are eliminated or distorted in the film?

- Compare the film with other films, books, and articles on the same subject.

3b-5 Single-source analysis

As noted in Chapter 2, primary sources comprise the basic materials of historical research. Because examining and interpreting primary sources is so fundamental to the historian's craft, many professors ask their students to write an analysis of a single primary source.

A single-source paper can take many forms. You may be asked to analyze a book-length text, a shorter document such as a letter, an artifact such as a tribal mask, or an image such as a photograph. You may be assigned a particular source to analyze, or you may be allowed to write about a source of your choosing. Whatever the specifics of your assignment, a single-source analysis asks you to examine a primary source in depth, often without reference to the work of other historians, in order to determine what it can tell you about the people and the period you are studying.

In order to write an effective primary source analysis, you will first need to ask questions about the nature of the source itself: Who wrote this document or made this artifact? When was this source created, and why? The questions for evaluating primary sources listed in the Tips for Writers boxes in Chapter 2, pages 11 and 12–13, will help you begin to think about the fundamental aspects of your source.

Once you have answered the basic questions about your source, however, you must go beyond simple description and discuss the *significance* of the source: What can it tell us about the person who wrote or made it, or the time and place in which he or she lived? Can the source tell us anything about the structures and norms of the author's society? What a source can tell you depends on both the nature of the source itself and the questions you ask of it. Think of yourself as a detective interrogating a witness who is not very forthcoming. The source you are analyzing can tell you quite a bit about the period and people you are studying, but not all of that information is obvious at first glance, and the "witness" might not volunteer everything it knows until you ask the right questions. In general, the quality of your source analysis will depend on the quality of the questions you ask; take enough time to read the document or examine the artifact carefully and extract from it every bit of information you can.

Finally, remember that a single-source analysis, like any other history paper, should focus on a thesis—the conclusion you have reached about the significance of the source as a result of your careful reading and analysis. (For more on developing and supporting a thesis, see 4c and 4d.)

3b-6 Historiographic essays

As noted in Chapter 1, historians frequently disagree about how to interpret the events they study. For example, some historians have interpreted the Magna Carta, a charter signed by King John of England in 1215, as a revolutionary declaration of fundamental individual freedoms; others have seen it as a conservative restatement of feudal privilege. These differences in interpretation reflect the varying approaches that historians take to their subject. For example, individual historians might be primarily interested in social, cultural, political, economic, legal, or intellectual history. They might approach their work from a Marxist, Freudian, feminist, or postmodernist point of view. Such orientations and affiliations affect the ways in which historians explore and interpret the past; thus, historians interested in the same historical event might examine different sets of sources to answer the same question. For example, in studying the causes of the French Revolution, Marxist historians might focus on economic and class issues, while intellectual historians might concentrate on how the writings of the philosophes (a group of French Enlightenment writers) affected political thought and practice. Moreover, since the historian's work is embedded in a particular social and cultural context, historical interpretations and methodologies change over time. For example, the growth of the civil rights and feminist movements in the 1960s led to a greater interest in African American and women's history. In order to make students aware of a variety of interpretations and allow them to enter the exciting world of historical discussion and debate, some instructors ask their students to write historiographic essays.

A historiographic essay is one in which the writer, acting as a historian, studies the approaches to a topic that other historians have taken. When you write a historiographic essay, you identify, compare, and evaluate the viewpoints of two or more historians writing on the same subject. Such an essay can take several forms. You might be asked, for example, to study the work of historians who lived during or near the time in which a particular event happened—for example, to explore the ways in which contemporary Chinese historians wrote about the Boxer Rebellion. A different kind of historiographic essay might require that you look at the ways in which historians have treated the same topic over time. For example, to examine how historians have treated Thomas Jefferson, you might begin with two pre–Civil War biographies—Matthew L. Davis's *Memoirs of Aaron Burr* (1836–37), which provides a scathing critique of Jefferson, and Henry S. Randall's contrastingly positive *Life of Jefferson* (1858)—and end with the most recent studies of Jefferson. Yet another such assignment might ask you to compare the views of historians from several historical schools on the same event. You might, for example, be asked to compare Whig and Progressive interpretations of the American Revolution or Marxist and feminist views of the French Revolution. Historiographic essays may be short or quite lengthy. In any case, a historiographic essay focuses attention not on a historical event itself but rather on how historians have interpreted that event.

A historiographic essay combines some of the features of a book review with those of a short essay or research paper. You should begin with a critical reading of the texts containing historians' interpretations, keeping in mind the questions you would need to answer if you were going to write book reviews about them (see 3b-3). You should not, however, treat the historiographic essay as two or three book reviews glued together. Rather, you should synthesize your material and construct an argument in support of a thesis. The following thesis is from a student's essay on historians' interpretations of the colonial period of African history:

> Historians have held dramatically different views about the impor-
> tance of European colonial rule in Africa: Marxist historians, along
> with others who focus on economic issues, have tended to see the
> colonial period as an important turning point, while cultural histo-
> rians have maintained that the impact of the West on the ancient
> cultural traditions of Africa was superficial.

In the rest of the paper, the student supports the thesis
as he or she would do in any other history paper. (For a
fuller discussion of formulating and supporting a thesis,
see 4c and 4d.)

3c   Taking history exams

History exams reflect your ability to synthesize the materials you have examined over the course of a semester
into a coherent picture of the period you are studying. If
you have been attending classes and reading actively and
critically throughout the semester, the final exam should
not be an occasion for panic but rather a chance to demonstrate your understanding of the people, events, and
institutions you have been studying.

History exams can follow many different formats. One
typical component of a history exam that allows the professor to evaluate the students' basic mastery of the material is a series of identification questions that ask students
to briefly describe and note the significance of important
persons, places, or events. Many instructors also test their
students' ability to synthesize the material they have been
studying throughout the semester by asking them to write
short essays that discuss a particular historical question or
issue in some detail. Since history exams can vary widely
in format, it is important to pay careful attention to your
professor's specific instructions. The following general
advice, which includes strategies for answering identification questions and composing short essays, can help you
prepare for any history exam.

3c-1   Preparing for an exam

The best preparation for an exam does not begin the
day, or even the week, before the exam but takes place
throughout the semester. Careful reading of the texts and

periodic review of your notes will ensure that you have a firm grasp of the material come exam time. Throughout the semester, you should do the following:

Attend class regularly and take good notes. It is not necessary to write down *everything* your professor says. When taking notes, you should listen for the main points and note the evidence given to support those points. (You will discover that your professor's lectures usually follow the same format as a good essay.) Follow the same suggestions for a discussion class; your classmates will often make important points about the material you are studying.

Review your notes regularly, preferably after each class. If you review your notes while the class is fresh in your mind, it will be easier for you to notice places where the notes are unclear. Mark these places, and clarify confusing points as soon as possible, either by researching the issue yourself or by asking your professor.

Keep a list of important ideas, people, and events. As you read your texts and review your class notes, it is useful to make a list of significant persons, places, events, and concepts along with a brief description of why they are important. Look up the definitions of terms with which you are unfamiliar. This not only will ensure that you understand the key ideas in the material you are studying but also will be particularly useful if your exam for the course includes an identification section. How do you know which items to include on this list? Some will be obvious; if you are taking a course called Twentieth-Century Dictators, it would be a good thing to be able to identify Hitler, Mussolini, and Stalin. In cases in which the importance of a person or an idea is not so obvious, look for other clues: words that are italicized in your texts; concepts that recur in several of your readings; and terms, events, or people that your professor has highlighted for you or written on the board.

Refer to your syllabus throughout the semester. Many instructors provide detailed syllabi that state the themes for each section of the course. Use the syllabus as a guide for your own studying and thinking about the course material.

Take careful notes on the reading.   Read with a notebook or computer at hand, and take notes as you read. Keep in mind that simply copying long sections from your texts is not very useful in ensuring that you have understood the material. It will be much more useful for you to take notes in the form of summaries. (See 3b-1 for a fuller discussion.)

Keep an academic journal.   Some professors require students to keep academic journals, but even if this is not the case for your class, you should consider doing so. In your journal, record important points about the material you are reading, any questions you want to answer or issues you would like to raise, important ideas suggested by class discussions, and so on. Use the journal to track your growing knowledge of the material you are studying.

The week before the exam, you should do the following:

Review your notes, syllabus, and texts.   Identify the most important themes and issues of the course, and assemble the evidence that clarifies those themes.

Anticipate questions.   Imagine that you are the professor faced with the task of creating the exam for this course. What questions would you ask? Framing your own exam questions and answering them can be a useful way of organizing your thoughts.

3c-2   Answering identification questions

Professors often use identification questions as a way of testing your basic understanding of the material covered in the course. You may be asked to identify people, places, or events, or to define important concepts. If you have kept a running list of significant individuals, events, and terms, you probably will not be surprised by any of the items in the identification section of your test.

   When answering identification questions, it is important to *read the directions carefully*. Students tend to make one of two mistakes in answering identification questions. On the one hand, they may produce answers that are too detailed. The response to an identification question should not be a fully developed, multi-page essay. So how much should you write? Often, your professor will tell you how long your response should be; you might, for example, be asked to write one sentence or a three- to four-sentence paragraph. The number of points an identification answer is worth also provides a clue to how much time you should spend writing your response. If your exam includes an essay worth 50 points, and ten identifications worth 5 points each, you obviously should not spend thirty minutes on one identification.

On the other hand, take care not to write too little. Your answer should be detailed enough to identify the individual person, event, or concept. Again, if each identification is worth 5 points, merely identifying Anne Boleyn as an English queen is clearly not enough; dozens of people can be identified as English queens. A more successful response would identify Anne Boleyn as the English queen who was the second wife of Henry VIII and the mother of Queen Elizabeth I. Moreover, identification questions may ask you to go one step further by noting the significance of the person, event, or concept. Sometimes, this expectation is spelled out in the directions with such wording as "identify and *explain the significance of* . . ." At other times, the suggested length of your answer provides the clue; if you are asked to write three to four sentences, you will need to provide more than a minimal identification. In this instance, thinking about why your professor has asked you to identify particular persons, events, or concepts will help you formulate your answer.

3c-3 Taking an essay exam

The essays you write for an exam will necessarily be shorter than the papers you write for your course, but they should follow the same basic format. In other words, an exam essay should begin with a thesis stated clearly in the first paragraph, followed by several paragraphs in which you provide evidence supporting your thesis, and end with a conclusion. (For detailed advice on writing a history essay, see Chapter 4.) The difficulty, of course, is that you will be writing this essay under pressure, in a limited period of time, and without the opportunity to check the accuracy of your data. The following are some suggestions for writing a successful essay on a history exam.

Preparing to write. *Do not begin to write right away.* This is probably the biggest mistake that students make in essay exams. Before you write, do the following:

- Read the exam carefully. Make sure you understand what each question is really asking. You will not gain points by scribbling down everything you know about the development of Chinese politics from the tenth century through the fifteenth century when the question asks you to discuss the impact of the Mongol invasion in 1260.

- If you are offered a choice, make sure you answer the question you can answer best. This may not always be the one you are drawn to first. One great insight about the significance of the Treaty of Waitangi will not be enough to write a good essay about Maori-British relations in nineteenth-century New Zealand. Be sure that you can cite several pieces of evidence in support of your thesis.

- Take the time to organize your thoughts. Jot down a quick outline for your essay, stating the thesis and listing the evidence you will provide to support that thesis.

Writing the essay.   Once you are ready to write, your essay should follow the same format as any other history essay:

- Begin by stating your thesis. *Do not* waste time restating the question; your professor knows what he or she asked.

- Cite the evidence that supports your thesis. If you are aware of any counterevidence, make sure you discuss it. (See 4d-2 for a discussion of counterevidence and how to deal with it.)

- Be sure you stick to the point. Do not go off on interesting tangents that are irrelevant to the question. Referring frequently to your outline will help keep you on track.

- Tie your essay together by stating your conclusions.

4
Writing History Papers

Each academic discipline has its own practices, or conventions, that people writing in the discipline follow when engaged in a scholarly dialogue. Following the conventions for writing in history will make it easier for you to participate in an academic conversation in your field. Moreover, many historians are excellent stylists. Your instructor will pay attention to your writing, so your attempts to learn and follow the conventions of the discipline will be noticed—and worth the effort.

History students are most often asked to write two types of papers: short essays and research papers. Unlike most of the assignments described in Chapter 3, such papers often require you to examine *multiple* (rather than single) sources. Writing a historical essay is a process of synthesis—pulling together different sources, thinking about their relationship, and drawing conclusions about what, taken together, they can tell you about your subject. This chapter provides advice on all aspects of writing short essays—relatively brief papers with limited sources and, frequently, an assigned topic. Full-fledged research papers, which build on the techniques outlined here, are considered in Chapter 5.

4a Approaching a history assignment

When faced with the task of writing a short essay in history, you must first analyze the assignment carefully, making sure to identify and understand *all* of its parts so that you know exactly what you are being asked to do. Some assignments include very specific and detailed directions, but in many cases the instructor's expectations will be implied, not explicit. To ensure that you fully understand your assignment, you should always do the following:

Determine the key verb. Most assignments include a key verb that will let you know how your instructor expects you to approach the essay. The following example is from a course on the history of Christian-Muslim relations:

> Compare the ways in which Fulcher of Chartres (a medieval Christian historian) and Ibn al-Athir (a medieval Muslim historian) explain the Christian success at the siege of Antioch during the First Crusade.

The operative word in the assignment is *compare*. Other assignments may ask you to *trace* the causes or *assess* the importance of a historical event. The key verb tells you how to structure your essay. For instance, an assignment that requires you to *compare* two or more texts, like the example given above, implies that you should give approximately equal weight to each of the sources included in your assignment, consider not only similarities but also differences, and come to some conclusion about the *significance* of the similarities and differences you have identified.

Determine what sources you should or may use. Short-paper assignments usually include specific instructions about which sources you should consider and, sometimes, which ones you may not. You might, for example, be instructed to consider *only* a specific set of newspaper articles or to develop your own interpretation of an artifact without reference to additional secondary sources. Always make sure you understand and follow these instructions.

Analyze and synthesize your sources. When you write a paper, you must, of course, begin by evaluating and analyzing each source you are using, following the advice given in 3a and 3b. For the assignment given above, for instance, you would need to understand what both Fulcher of Chartres *and* Ibn al-Athir thought about the siege of Antioch.

Analyzing each source, though, is not sufficient; you also need to synthesize the information in your sources by identifying specific points of comparison. When you use several sources as a means for interpreting a historical event, you should take care to integrate evidence from each source throughout your paper. An essay for the above assignment, for example, should *not* take the form of two mini-papers—one on Fulcher and one on Ibn al-Athir—glued together. Rather, it should examine the two sources *as they relate to each other*. You might discover, for example, that Fulcher and Ibn al-Athir agree that the gates to the city were opened for the Christian army by a Muslim cuirass-maker, but that they differ in their interpretation of this event: Ibn al-Athir reports that the traitor succumbed to bribery, while Fulcher maintains that his actions were the result of three divine visions.

Finally, keep in mind that merely reporting the content of a text or texts, or providing a laundry list of similarities and differences, does not constitute a history essay; underlying every essay assignment in history is the question "Why is this important?" In the sample assignment, the instructor's expectation is that the student will not only analyze both sources and identify their similarities and differences but also draw conclusions about the *meaning* of those similarities and differences and explain why they are *significant*. You might note, for example, that the two texts provide very different perspectives on causation in history: the Christian historian ascribes almost everything that happened during the siege to the direct action of God, whereas the Muslim historian explains the same events without reference to divine intervention. One approach to writing this essay, then, might be to consider the degree to which medieval authors from different religious cultures shared a common set of beliefs about the world: What ideas do they share, and how and why do their worldviews differ?

Stay on topic. Be careful to write about the topic that has actually been assigned. In reading Fulcher and Ibn al-Athir, for example, you may discover that both authors discuss the importance of Jerusalem in their respective religions. Although this is an interesting and important topic, it is not the subject of the assignment.

4b Thinking like a historian

Before you begin to write your essay, you need to become familiar with a number of conventions that historians have established to govern their relationship with their subject; in other words, you need to learn how to think like a historian. Learning these conventions will enable you to be an active participant in historical conversations.

Respect your subject.   When you write a history paper, you are forming a relationship of sorts with real people and events whose integrity must be respected. The people who lived in the past were not necessarily more ignorant or cruel (or, conversely, more innocent or moral) than we are. It is condescending, for example, to suggest that an intelligent or insightful person was "ahead of his or her time" (suggesting, of course, that he or she thought the same way we do).

Do not generalize.   Remember that groups are formed of individuals. Do not assume that everyone who lived in the past believed the same things or behaved the same way. Avoid broad generalizations such as "the medieval period was an Age of Faith" or "pre-modern people were not emotionally attached to their children." At best, such statements are clichés. More often than not, they are also wrong. (For more on the issue of appropriate language, see 4g-1.)

Avoid anachronism.   An anachronistic statement is one in which an idea, event, person, or thing is represented in a way that is not consistent with its proper historical time or context. For example, "Despite the fact that bubonic plague can be controlled with antibiotics, medieval physicians treated their patients with ineffective folk remedies." This sentence includes two anachronisms. First, although antibiotics are effective against bubonic plague, they had not yet been discovered in the fourteenth century; it is anachronistic to mention them in a discussion of the Middle Ages. Second, it is anachronistic to judge medieval medicine by modern standards. A more effective discussion of the medieval response to the bubonic plague would focus on fourteenth-century knowledge about health and disease, theories of contagion, and sanitation practices. In short, you should not import the values, beliefs, and practices of the present into the past. Try to understand the people and events of the past in their own contexts.

Be aware of your own biases.   We naturally choose to write about subjects that interest us. Historians should not, however, let their own concerns and biases direct the way they interpret the past. A student of early modern Europe, for example, might be dismayed by the legal, social, and economic limitations placed on women in that period. Reproaching sixteenth-century men for being "selfish and chauvinistic" might forcefully express such a student's sense of indignation about what appears to modern eyes as unjust, but it is not a useful approach for the historian, who tries to understand the viewpoints of people in the past in the social context of the period under study.

4c   Developing a thesis

Your *topic* is the subject you have been assigned to write about (for example, the Salem witchcraft trials, the Lewis and Clark expedition, the rise of the Nazi party). If you merely collect bits of information about your topic, however, you will not have written an effective history paper. A history paper, like many other kinds of academic writing, usually takes the form of an argument in support of a *thesis*—a statement that reflects the conclusion you have reached about your topic after a careful analysis of the sources.

Since the thesis is the central idea that drives a history essay, it is important that you understand exactly what a thesis is. Imagine that you have been given the following essay assignment:

> Discuss the role of nonviolent resistance in the Indian independence movement.

As you develop your thesis statement, keep the following in mind:

- **A thesis is *not* a description of your paper topic.** Although your reader should not have to guess what your paper is about, the thesis must do more than announce your subject or the purpose for which you are writing. "This paper is about the role of nonviolent resistance in the Indian independence movement" is *not* a thesis statement; nor is "The purpose of this paper is to describe the methods Mohandas Gandhi used to gain Indian independence from Great Britain." These sentences merely restate the assigned topic.

- **A thesis is *not* a question.** Although historians always ask questions as they read (see 3a for advice on active reading) and a thesis statement arises from the historian's attempt to answer a question, a question is not, in itself, a thesis. "Why were Mohandas Gandhi's methods successful in the movement to achieve Indian independence from Great Britain?" is a valid historical question, but it is *not* a thesis statement.

- **A thesis is *not* a statement of fact.** While historians deal in factual information about the past, a fact, however interesting, is simply a piece of data. The statement "Mohandas Gandhi led the movement for Indian independence from Britain" is *not* a thesis.

- **A thesis is *not* a statement of opinion.** Although a thesis statement must reflect what you have concluded, it cannot be a simple statement of belief or preference. The assertion "Mohandas Gandhi is my favorite political leader of the twentieth century" does *not* constitute a thesis.

In short, a thesis is *not* a description of your paper topic, a question, a statement of fact, or a statement of opinion, although it is sometimes confused with all of the above. Rather, *a thesis is a statement that reflects what you have concluded about the topic of your paper, based on a critical analysis and interpretation of the source materials you have examined.*

For the assignment given above, the following sentence *is* an acceptable thesis:

> From the moment that Mohandas Gandhi decided to respond to force with acts of civil disobedience, British rule of India was doomed; his indictment of British colonial policy in the court of public opinion did far more damage to the British military than any weapon could.

You should note three things about this statement. First, while the thesis is not itself a question, it *is* an answer to a question—in this case, the question posed above: "Why were Mohandas Gandhi's methods successful in the movement to achieve Indian independence from Great Britain?" A thesis usually arises from the questions you pose of the text or texts as you engage in active reading. Second, the thesis is *specific.* In attempting to answer the historical question raised above, the writer did not make a broad generalization like "Gandhi was successful because people thought he was a good person" or "Gandhi succeeded because the British were treating the Indians badly." Rather, the thesis makes a specific claim: that the contrast between Gandhi's use of civil disobedience and the use of force by the British had a significant impact on public opinion. Third, a thesis is always a debatable point, a *conclusion* with which a thoughtful reader might disagree. In other words, the thesis makes an assertion that sets up an *argument*. It is the writer's job, in the body of a paper, to provide an argument based on evidence that will convince the reader that his or her thesis is a valid one. The thesis, then, is the heart of your paper. It presents what you have concluded about the topic under discussion and provides the focal point for the rest of the essay.

To ensure that your thesis really is a thesis, review the Tips for Writers box on page 46.

4d   Constructing an argument

One reason you might find it difficult to develop a thesis statement is that you feel hesitant to come to independent conclusions about the meaning and significance of the materials you are working with; after all, what if your interpretation is wrong? It often seems safer just to reiterate the topic, or ask a question, or state a fact with which no one could argue. But, as noted in 4c, to write an effective history paper, you must be willing to reach a conclusion about your subject that could be challenged or debated by an intelligent reader. While this may seem intimidating, keep in mind that historical issues are seldom clear-cut and that professional historians, working from the same sources, often disagree with each other or form different interpretations. It is unlikely that there is only one correct point of view concerning the topic you have been assigned or only one correct interpretation of the sources you are examining. You do not need to convince your readers that your thesis or argument represents the only possible interpretation of the evidence. You do, however, need to convince them that your interpretation is valid. You will be able to do this only if you have provided concrete evidence from reliable sources in support of your argument and have responded honestly to opposing positions.

Tips for Writers
Testing Your Thesis

If . . .		Then . . .
Your proposed thesis does no more than repeat the topic you are writing about	→	It is *not* a thesis.
Your proposed thesis poses a question without suggesting an answer	→	It is *not* a thesis.
Your proposed thesis merely articulates a fact or series of facts	→	It is *not* a thesis.
Your proposed thesis simply reflects a personal belief or preference	→	It is *not* a thesis.

BUT

If . . .		Then . . .
Your proposed thesis: • suggests an answer to a question you have posed as a result of your reading, *and* • is specific, rather than general, *and* • is debatable (that is, it asserts a conclusion with which a reader might disagree), *and* • can be supported by evidence from the sources	→	It *is* a thesis.

4d-1 Supporting your thesis

To support your argument, you must offer evidence from your sources. Imagine that you have been given the following assignment in a course on the history of science: "Analyze the role played by experiment and observation in William Harvey's *On the Motion of the Heart and Blood in Animals*." A student writing an essay on this topic would have noticed that Harvey describes his experimental method and his observations in great detail. She would also have noticed, however, that Harvey drew inspiration from the analogy he saw between the sun as the center of the solar system and the heart as the center of the body, and that this analogy led him to consider whether the blood, like the planets, might move about the body in a circular motion. Her thesis will depend on the conclusion she has reached, after careful and active reading of the text, about which of these elements was more significant in his discovery of circulation. If she concludes that experimentation and observation were more important in Harvey's thinking, her thesis statement might look like this:

> Although Harvey sometimes used analogies and symbols in his discussion of the movement of the heart and the blood, it was his careful observations, his elegantly designed experiments, and his meticulous measurements that led him to discover circulation.

If, on the other hand, she concluded that Harvey's philosophical commitments were more significant, she might write the following:

> Harvey's commitment to observation and experiment mark him as one of the fathers of the modern scientific method; however, a careful reading of *On the Motion of the Heart and Blood in Animals* suggests that the idea of circulation did not arise simply from the scientific elements of his thinking, but was inspired by his immersion in neo-Platonic philosophy.

Note that the writer of this essay could come to *either* of these conclusions after a careful examination of the text. What is essential is that the student support her thesis by constructing an argument with evidence taken from the text itself. It is *not* enough simply to make an assertion and expect readers to agree. In the first instance, she would support her thesis by pointing to examples of experiments Harvey designed and carried out. She might also note Harvey's emphasis on quantification and the care with which he described experiments that could be replicated. In the second instance, she might note the number of times Harvey compares the heart to the sun, thus providing an analogy for circulation. She might also note that Harvey was unable to observe circulation directly, since capillaries are too small to be seen with the microscopes available at the time, and that his belief in circulation therefore required an intuitive leap that could not have been drawn solely from observation or experiment. In both cases, the student would cite *specific* instances from the text to support her thesis, integrating quotes from the source as appropriate. (For more on using quotations, see 7a-2.)

4d-2 Responding to counterevidence and anticipating opposing viewpoints

Acknowledging counterevidence—source data that does not support your argument—will not weaken your paper. On the contrary, if you address counterevidence effectively, you strengthen your argument by showing why it is legitimate despite information that seems to contradict it. If, for example, the student writing about Harvey wanted to argue for the primacy of experiment and observation in his work, she would need to show that these elements were more significant than his interest in philosophical speculation. If she wanted to argue that his philosophy was more important, she would have to demonstrate that it was his keen interest in the ways in which some philosophers interpreted the centrality of the sun in the universe as a metaphor that allowed him to interpret what he observed about the movement of the blood and the heart in creative new ways. In either case, her argument would need to be based on a consideration of the evidence and counterevidence contained in the relevant source or sources, not merely on her own gut feelings.

Similarly, if you are writing an essay in which you are examining secondary sources, you should demonstrate that you are aware of the work of historians whose interpretations differ from your own; never simply ignore an argument that doesn't support your interpretation. It is perfectly legitimate to disagree with others' interpretations; this is, after all, one of the purposes of writing a book review or a historiographic essay (see 3b-3 and 3b-6). In disagreeing, however, it is important to treat opposing viewpoints with respect; you should never resort to name-calling, oversimplifying, or otherwise distorting opposing points of view. *Your essay will be stronger, not weaker, if you understand opposing arguments and respond to them fairly.*

A good argument, then, does not ignore evidence or arguments that seem to contradict or weaken the thesis. If you discover information that does not support your thesis, do not suppress it. It is important to acknowledge *all* of your data. Try to explain to readers why your interpretation is valid, despite the existence of counter-evidence or alternative arguments, but do not imply that your interpretation is stronger than it is by eliminating data or falsifying information. Rather, a successful paper would respond to counterevidence and differing interpretations by addressing them directly and explaining why, in your view, they do not negate your thesis.

Note: Of course, if the counterevidence is too strong, you will need to adjust, or even completely change, your thesis. Always be open to the possibility that your initial conclusions might need to be modified in response to the evidence you find. (For more on the process of gathering evidence and developing a thesis, see 5b.)

4e Organizing your paper

Even after analyzing an assignment, reading the sources carefully with a historian's eyes, developing a thesis, and finding evidence in the sources that supports your thesis, you may still find it difficult to organize your ideas into an effective paper. History papers, like other academic writings, include an introduction, a body, and a conclusion. This section examines the specific elements that your history instructor will expect to find in each of these parts of your paper.

4e-1 Drafting an introduction

The introductory paragraph of your paper is in many ways the most important one and therefore the most difficult to write. In your introduction, you must (1) let your readers know what your paper is about and provide background information on the texts, people, or problems under discussion; (2) put the topic of your paper into context; and (3) state your thesis. You must also attract your readers' attention and interest. The opening paragraph, then, has to frame the rest of the paper and make readers want to continue reading. There is no magic formula for writing an effective first paragraph. You should, however, keep the following conventions in mind.

Do not open with a global statement. Unsure of how to start, many students begin their papers with phrases like "Throughout history . . ." or "From the beginning of time . . ." or "People have always wondered about . . ." You should avoid generalizations like these. First, you cannot prove that they are true: How do you know what people have always thought or done? Second, these statements are so broad that they are virtually meaningless; they offer no specific points or details to interest readers. Finally, such statements are so vague that they give readers no clue about the subject of your paper. It is much more effective to begin with material specific to your topic.

The following opening sentence comes from the first draft of a student paper on William Harvey's *On the Motion of the Heart and Blood in Animals*:

INEFFECTIVE

From ancient times, people have always been interested in the human body and how it works.

Although, grammatically, there is nothing wrong with this sentence, it is not a particularly effective opening. For one thing, it is such a general statement that readers will be inclined to ask, "So what?" In addition, it gives readers no indication of what the paper is about. Will the essay examine ancient Greek medical theory? Chinese acupuncture? Sex education in twentieth-century American schools?

In revising the sentence, the student eliminated the general statement altogether and began instead with a description of the intellectual context of Harvey's work:

EFFECTIVE

For the scholars and physicians of seventeenth-century Europe, observation and experimentation began to replace authoritative texts as the most important source of information about human anatomy and physiology.

From this one sentence, readers learn four things about the subject of the paper: the time frame of the discussion (the seventeenth century), the place (Europe), the people involved (scholars and physicians), and the topic (the importance of experiment and observation in the biological sciences). Readers' curiosity is also piqued by the questions the sentence implies: Why did experimentation begin to replace authoritative texts? Was this change a subject of controversy? Who was involved? How did this change in method affect the science of biology and the practice of medicine? In other words, this opening sentence makes readers want to continue reading; they want to know the author's thesis.

Include your thesis in the first paragraph. If your opening sentence has been effective, it will make your readers want to know the main point of your paper, which you will state in the thesis. As you read works by professional historians, you may notice that the introduction to a journal article or book may be long, even several paragraphs, and the author's thesis may appear anywhere within it. Until you become skilled in writing about history, however, it is best to keep your introduction short and to state your thesis in the first paragraph. The following is the first draft of the introductory paragraph for the paper on Harvey:

INEFFECTIVE

From ancient times, people have always been interested in the human body and how it works. Harvey was a seventeenth-century physician who performed many experiments and discovered the circulation of the blood.

This introduction begins with the ineffective opening sentence we looked at above. The "thesis statement" that follows isn't really a thesis at all; it is simply a statement of fact. (For more on writing an effective thesis, see 4c.) Moreover, there is no clear connection established between the ideas contained in the opening sentence and Harvey. From this first paragraph, a reader would have no idea what the paper was about, what its central point might be, or what to expect in the pages that follow.

In the final version of this introductory paragraph, the student uses the revised opening sentence and incorporates a more effective thesis, which is underlined here:

EFFECTIVE

For the scholars and physicians of seventeenth-century Europe, observations and experimentation began to replace authoritative texts as the most important source of information about human anatomy and physiology. This trend is clearly illustrated in the work of William Harvey, who designed controlled experiments to measure blood flow. However, Harvey was not led to his revolutionary discovery of the circulation of the blood by experimentation alone, but was inspired by flashes of intuition and philosophical speculation.

In this introductory paragraph, the connection between Harvey and the rise of observation and experiment in the seventeenth century is clear. Moreover, the thesis statement reflects the author's conclusions and anticipates the argument that will follow; we can expect that in the course of the paper, the author will support her argument by discussing Harvey's experimental method, his philosophical speculations, his moments of intuition, and the role all three played in his theories about circulation.

Plan to rewrite your opening paragraph.   Because the opening paragraph plays such a crucial role in the overall effectiveness of your paper, you should always plan on revising it several times. In addition, when the paper is complete, it is important to check each section against the introduction. Does each paragraph provide evidence for your thesis? Is it clear to your reader how each point relates to the topic you have established in your introduction? Knowing that you will have to rewrite your introduction can be reassuring if you are having trouble beginning your paper. Write a rough, temporary opening paragraph, and return to it when you finish your first draft of the entire paper. The act of writing your draft will help you clarify your ideas, your topic, and your thesis.

4e-2   Writing clear and connected paragraphs

In your introduction, you present your subject and state your thesis. In the body of your paper, you provide an argument for your thesis based on evidence from the sources you have been reading and answer any objections that could be raised. You should think of each paragraph as a building block in your argument that presents one specific point. If the point of each paragraph is not clear, the reader will not be able to follow your reasoning and your paper will be weak and unconvincing. (For more on constructing an argument, see 4d.) The following advice will help you write well-organized, cohesive, and persuasive paragraphs.

Begin each paragraph with a topic sentence.   Each paragraph should have one driving idea that provides support for your paper's overall thesis. This idea is usually asserted in the *topic sentence*. If you have made an outline, your topic sentences will be drawn from your list of the main points you wish to cover in your paper. (For advice on making an outline, see 5e.)

Provide support for the paragraph's main point. The topic sentence should be followed by *evidence* in the form of examples, quotations from the text(s), or statistics that support the main point of the paragraph. Make sure that you do not wander off the point. If you include irrelevant information, you will lose momentum and your readers will lose the thread of your argument. Instead, make sure you choose examples that provide clear and sufficient support for your main point. If you are using a direct quote as evidence, make sure you explain to the reader why you are including this quote by integrating it grammatically into your text and framing it in a way that shows how it supports your point. (For more information on how and when to quote, see 7a.)

Make clear connections between ideas. To be convincing, your evidence must be clear and well organized. Transitional words and phrases tell your readers how the individual statements in your paragraph are connected. To choose transitions that are appropriate, you will need to think about how your ideas are related. The following are some transitional words or phrases that indicate particular kinds of relationships:

- **To compare:** *also, similarly, likewise.*
- **To contrast:** *on the one hand/on the other hand, although, conversely, nevertheless, despite, on the contrary, still, yet, regardless, nonetheless, notwithstanding, whereas, however, in spite of.*
- **To add or intensify:** *also, in addition, moreover, further, too, besides, and.*
- **To show sequence:** *first* (and any other ordinal number), *last, next, finally, subsequently, later, ultimately.*
- **To indicate an example:** *for example, for instance, specifically.*
- **To indicate cause-and-effect relationships:** *consequently, as a result, because, accordingly, thus, since, therefore, so.*

Writing paragraphs: an example. The following is a paragraph from the first draft of a paper on Chinese relationships with foreigners during the Ming period:

INEFFECTIVE

The Chinese were willing to trade with barbarians. They distrusted foreigners. Jesuit missionaries were able to establish contacts in China. During the seventeenth century, they acquired the patronage of important officials. They were the emperor's advisers. Chinese women bound their feet, a practice that many Europeans disliked. Relations between China and Europe deteriorated in the eighteenth century. The Jesuits were willing to accommodate themselves to Chinese culture. Chinese culture was of great interest to the scholars of Enlightenment Europe. Matteo Ricci learned about Chinese culture and became fluent in Mandarin. He adopted the robes of a Chinese scholar. He thought that Christianity was compatible with Confucianism. The Jesuit missionaries had scientific knowledge.

Although each sentence is grammatically correct, this paragraph as a whole is very confusing. In the first place, it has no clear topic sentence; readers have to guess what the writer's main point is. This confusion is compounded by unclear connections between ideas; the paragraph lacks transitional words or phrases that alert readers to the connections that the writer sees between ideas or events. The paragraph is also poorly organized; the writer seems to move at random from topic to topic.

The following is a revised version of the same paragraph:

EFFECTIVE

<u>The Chinese of the Ming dynasty were deeply suspicious of foreigners;</u> <u>*nevertheless*, Jesuit missionaries were able to achieve positions of</u> <u>honor and trust in the imperial court, ultimately serving the emperor</u> <u>as scholars and advisers.</u> *At first glance*, this phenomenon seems baffling; upon closer consideration, *however*, it becomes clear that the Jesuits' success was due to their willingness to accommodate themselves to Chinese culture. *For example*, one of the most successful of the early Jesuit missionaries, Matteo Ricci, steeped himself in Chinese culture *and* became fluent in Mandarin. To win the respect of the nobles, he *also* adopted the robes of a Chinese scholar. *Moreover*, he emphasized the similarities between Christianity and Chinese traditions. *Because* of their willingness to adapt to Chinese culture, Jesuit missionaries were accepted by the imperial court until the eighteenth century.

This paragraph has been improved in several ways. First, a topic sentence (which is underlined) has been added to th beginning. Readers no longer need to guess that this paragraph will address the apparent contrast between sixteenth-century Chinese suspicion of foreigners and the imperial court's acceptance of Jesuit missionaries.

Second, the author has clarified the connections between ideas by including transitional words and phrases. These transitions (which are italicized) illustrate several different kinds of relationships—including contrast, cause and effect, and sequence—and allow readers to follow the writer's argument.

Third, the paragraph has been reorganized so that the relationships between events are clearer. For example, the revised paragraph states explicitly that the Jesuits' adaptation to Chinese customs was the key reason for the success of European missionaries during the Ming dynasty; this connection is obscured in the original paragraph by poor organization. Finally, the writer has removed references to foot binding and to European interest in China during the Enlightenment. Both are interesting but irrelevant in a paragraph that deals with Chinese attitudes toward Europeans.

4e-3 Writing an effective conclusion

Your paper should not come to an abrupt halt, yet you do not need to conclude by summarizing everything that you have said in the body of the text. An effective conclusion performs two vital functions. First, it brings the paper full circle by reminding the reader of the thesis and reiterating the *most important* points that were made in support of the thesis. Second, it answers the main question that your reader, having read the entire paper, will want to know: "Why is this important?" Thus, it is usually best to end your paper with a paragraph that states the most important conclusions you have reached about your subject and the reasons you think those conclusions are significant.

Note: A common pitfall for students is to end the paper with some new idea or fact. You should avoid introducing new ideas or information in the conclusion. If an idea or fact is important to your argument, you should introduce and discuss it earlier; if it is not, leave it out altogether.

The following is the first draft of the conclusion for the paper on Christian missionaries in China:

INEFFECTIVE

The Jesuit missionaries were sent to China in the Ming period. Some had good relationships with the emperor, but others didn't. Some learned Mandarin and dressed in court robes. The pope wouldn't let the Chinese worship their ancestors, but some Jesuits thought that Confucianism and Christianity were compatible. Another interesting aspect of Chinese culture at the time was the practice of footbinding.

This conclusion is ineffective for several reasons. First, there are no verbal clues to indicate that this is, in fact, the conclusion. In addition, it is too general and vague: Which missionaries had good relationships with the emperor, and which didn't? Moreover, while it lists some of the key elements of the paper, it fails to indicate how these ideas are connected. Most important, perhaps, this conclusion does not suggest why the various ideas presented in the paper are important; it fails, in other words, to answer the questions "So what? Why is this important?" Finally, a new topic is introduced in the last sentence.

In the revised version of the conclusion, these problems have been addressed:

EFFECTIVE

Thus, if we look at the experience of the Jesuits in China, it seems that their success or failure depended largely on the degree to which they were able to adapt to Chinese culture. The most successful missionaries learned Mandarin, adopted Chinese court dress, and looked for parallels between Christianity and the teachings of Confucius. It was only when the Church became more conservative — forbidding Chinese Christians, for example, to venerate their ancestors — that the Christian missionary effort in China began to fail. Ultimately, willingness to accept traditional Chinese culture and practices may have been a better way to gain converts than preaching complicated sermons.

This conclusion has been improved in several ways: It includes key transitional words (*thus, ultimately*) that indicate that the writer is drawing conclusions. It reiterates the important elements of the paper's argument but leaves out information that is either very general ("the Jesuit missionaries were sent to China in the Ming period") or too vague ("some had good relationships with the emperor, but others didn't"). Moreover, unlike the earlier version, it is explicit about how the key topics in the paper—the flexibility of the Jesuit missionaries in adapting to Chinese culture, the parallels the missionaries drew between Christianity and Confucianism, and the institution of more conservative policies—are related. It does not add any new topics, however interesting those topics might be. And, most important, this version, unlike the first draft, clearly outlines the significance of the conclusions that the writer has reached: The Jesuit experience in China tells us something about the relationship between culture and religious belief.

4f Revising for content and organization

One of the biggest mistakes you can make with any writing assignment is to leave yourself too little time to revise and edit your work. A paper written the night before it is due is never of the highest caliber and usually bears the hallmarks of careless writing: sloppy mistakes in reasoning, awkward constructions, poor word choice, and lack of clear organization. To write an effective history paper, you *must* allow yourself time to review your paper, preferably at least twice: once to revise it for content and organization, and once to edit it for sentence style and grammatical correctness. (For advice on editing for style and grammar, see 4g.)

The word *revise* comes from the Latin *revisere*, which means "to look at again." When you revise a paper, you are, quite literally, looking at the paper again with critical eyes. To begin revising your paper, you need to read it critically, as if it were someone else's work. (For advice on critical reading, see 3a.) You should read for logic and clarity, making sure that your evidence is sufficient and that it supports your thesis. Be ruthless: Eliminate all extraneous material from the final draft, however interesting it may be. For instance, if you are writing about the role that Chinese laborers played in the westward expansion of the American railroads, do not spend three paragraphs discussing the construction of the steam locomotive. If your paper concerns the American government's treatment

Tips for Writers
Revising for Content and Organization

- Does the first paragraph introduce the subject of the paper and provide information about the texts, people, or problems under discussion?
- Does the paper have a real thesis that is *specific* and *debatable*? Is the thesis clearly stated in the first paragraph?
- Does the paper provide sufficient evidence to support the thesis? Has counterevidence been carefully considered and addressed?
- Is the paper's argument clear and logical? Has the evidence from sources been synthesized into a cohesive structure?
- Have historical subjects been treated with respect? Does the paper avoid generalizations, anachronisms, and bias in both its language and its assumptions?
- Does each paragraph address one specific point, stated clearly in a topic sentence, and does each point support the paper's central argument?
- Is each paragraph clearly and logically organized? Do transitional words and phrases signal relationships within and between paragraphs?
- Has any irrelevant or extraneous material been eliminated?
- Does the conclusion tie the paper together?
- Is the paper properly documented? (See 6b and Chapter 7.)

of Japanese citizens during World War II, do not digress into a discussion of naval tactics in the Pacific theater. You must be willing to rearrange the order of material, do additional research to support weak points in your argument, and even change your entire thesis, if necessary. Obviously, you need to allow plenty of time for this part of the writing process, which may involve several drafts of the paper. The questions in the Tips for Writers box above will help you revise the content of your own paper or write an effective peer review for a classmate.

4g   Editing for style and grammar

Once you have finished revising your paper for matters of content and organization (see 4f), you are ready for editing, the final stage of the writing process, in which you focus on sentence style and grammatical correctness.

Although historians have long been just as concerned with proper grammar as English professors are, it is beyond the scope of this manual to cover the basic grammatical rules such as comma placement, subject-verb agreement, and pronoun usage. Grammar- and spell-check programs will help you avoid *some* mistakes, but they are no substitute for learning the rules. Also, a spell checker will not pick up words spelled correctly but used incorrectly or in the wrong context (for example, *Mink dynasty* instead of *Ming*). For advice on the basic rules of English grammar, you should buy, and use, a general writing guide. (See Appendix A for a list of guides.)

While you must follow grammatical rules, you *do* have some flexibility when it comes to style, or the way in which you write (simple vs. complex sentences, highly descriptive vs. stark wording). The way in which you express yourself and the words you choose are a reflection of your own style. Nevertheless, historians tend to follow certain conventions governing language, tense, and voice that you will want to keep in mind when you write and revise your history papers.

4g-1 Choosing appropriate language

Section 4b introduced you to some of the habits of mind that will help you think like a historian: you need to respect your subject, avoid generalization and anachronism, and be aware of your biases and assumptions. As you write and revise your paper, make sure that your writing demonstrates that you have adopted these good thinking practices.

Avoid value-laden words. Historians, as noted earlier in this chapter (see 4b), attempt to understand the people of the past in their own contexts rather than judge them by the norms of the present. If you use value-laden words such as *backward, primitive, uncivilized,* and *superstitious,* you are implying that your own period, culture, and perceptions are superior to those of the past. Passing judgment on the people of the past does not help us understand *what* they believed, *why* they believed it, or the social and cultural *context* in which they formed their beliefs.

Avoid biased language. Always take care to avoid words that are gender-biased or that have negative connotations for particular racial, ethnic, or religious groups. You should never use expressions that are clearly derogatory. In addition, you should be aware that many words that were once acceptable are now deemed inappropriate. For example, the use of masculine words to refer to both men and women, once a common practice, is now viewed as sexist by many. Use *humankind* or *people* rather than *mankind*, and do not use masculine pronouns when referring to people of both genders.

In an attempt to avoid sexist language, students sometimes make a grammatical error instead. For example, in trying to eliminate the masculine pronoun *his* in the sentence "Each individual reader should form *his* own opinion," a student may write, "Each individual reader should form *their* own opinion." The problem with this new version is that the pronoun *their* is plural, while the antecedent, *reader*, is singular. The first version of the sentence is undesirable because it sounds sexist, and the second is unacceptable because it is ungrammatical. A grammatically correct revision is "Individual readers should form their own opinions." In this sentence, the antecedent (*readers*) and the pronoun (*their*) are both plural.

Note that you cannot always rely on the books you are reading to alert you to biased language. In older publications, you may encounter previously common terms such as *Oriental* or *Negro* to refer to people, but these words are generally no longer used. Today, the preferred word for people of Asian heritage is *Asian*; people of African descent are generally called *black* or (for U.S. history) *African American*.

Note: You cannot correct the language of your sources. If you are quoting directly, you must use the exact wording of your source, including any racist or sexist language. If you are paraphrasing or summarizing a paragraph containing biased language, you might want to use unbiased language when it doesn't distort the sense of the source. Otherwise, put biased terms in quotation marks to indicate to your readers that the words are your source's and not yours.

Avoid conversational language, slang, and jargon. Because history papers are usually formal, you should use formal language rather than conversational language and slang. For example, although it is perfectly acceptable in conversational English to say that someone was a "major player" in an event, this expression is too informal for a history paper. In addition, slang often sounds anachronistic: Historians do not usually describe diplomats who fail to negotiate a treaty as having "struck out." Similarly, historians describe ideas as archaic or outdated, not "so two minutes ago." Words with double meanings should be used only in their conventional sense; use *sweet* to refer to taste and *radical* to describe something extreme or on the political left. *Awesome* should generally be reserved for awe-inspiring things like the Taj Mahal. You should also avoid jargon, or specialized language, which can often obscure your meaning.

Finally, contractions (such as *wasn't* for "was not" and *won't* for "will not") are generally too informal for use in a history paper. Rather, you should use the expanded form.

Make your language as clear and simple as possible. If you hope to convince your reader that your thesis is valid, he or she has to be able to understand what you are trying to say. The following suggestions will help ensure that your writing doesn't include elements that obscure your meaning.

- **Don't overuse your thesaurus.** In an effort to sound sophisticated, students sometimes use a thesaurus to try to find impressive words. The danger of this approach is that a new word might not mean what you intended.

- **Avoid pretentious-sounding words and phrases.** Use the simplest word that makes your meaning clear. Do not use a four-syllable word when a single syllable will do. Do not use five words (such as *due to the fact that*) where you can use one (*because*).

- **Avoid generalities.** Labels such as *college graduates*, *the poor*, *the Maori*, and *Protestants* create the impression that all members of a group think and behave in *exactly* the same manner. In reality, groups are comprised of individuals, each of whom is different and acts independently. Be as precise as possible: don't say "women" agitated for the vote when you mean "English suffragettes."

- **Replace vague references with specifics.** The use of phrases such as *other factors*, *additional forces*, or *outside influences* leaves the reader without necessary information. What, exactly, are these factors, forces, or influences? Vague references often disguise the writer's lack of information or clear thinking—a writer may use a phrase like *other factors* because he is not really sure what those factors are himself. Vague references not only obscure your meaning but can undermine your credibility.

- **Avoid unnecessarily wordy sentences.** Your writing will be more interesting if you use sentences of varying length; however, you should avoid overly long sentences with several dependent clauses. Your reader should not become so entangled in the sentence that she can no longer remember what the subject was by the time she reaches the verb! Try reading your sentences out loud; it is sometimes easier to hear sentences that are too long or confusing than to recognize them in print.

4g-2 Choosing the appropriate tense

The events that historians write about took place in the past; therefore, you should use the past tense when writing a history paper. Students are sometimes tempted to use the historical present tense for dramatic effect, as in this example from a student paper:

INEFFECTIVE

The battle rages all around him, but the squire is brave and acquits himself well. He defends his lord fearlessly and kills two of the enemy. As the fighting ends, he kneels before his lord on the battlefield, the bodies of the dead and dying all around him. His lord draws his sword and taps it against the squire's shoulders. The squire has proven his worth, and this is his reward; he is now a knight.

This use of the present tense may be an effective device if you are writing fiction, but it is awkward in a history paper. First, readers might become confused about whether the events under discussion happened in the past or in the present, especially if the paper includes modern assessments of the issue. Second, use of the present makes it easy for the writer to fall prey to anachronism (see 4b). Perhaps more important, writing in the present sounds artificial; in normal conversation, we talk about events that happened in the past in the past tense. The same approach is also best for writing.

Do use the present tense, however, when discussing the contents of documents, artifacts, or works of art because these still exist. Note, for example, the appropriate use of past and present tenses in the following description:

EFFECTIVE

Columbus sailed across an "ocean sea" far greater than he initially imagined. The admiral's *Journal* tells us what Columbus thought he would find: a shorter expanse of water, peppered with hundreds of hospitable islands.

The events of the past are referred to in the past tense (*sailed, imagined, thought*), and the contents of the *Journal* are referred to in the present (*tells*).

Historians also use the present tense when they are referring to the work of other scholars. Note, for example, this sentence from the annotated bibliography entry in Chapter 3: "Fletcher . . . argues that . . . Christians and Muslims did not achieve any real measure of mutual understanding in the period under discussion."

4g-3 Using active voice

In the *active voice*, the subject of the sentence is the actor. In the *passive voice*, the subject of the sentence is the object of the action; a passive sentence avoids naming an actor. In addition to making writing sound dull and unnecessarily wordy, the passive voice can lead to writing that is confusing, vague, and unassertive—characteristics that you will want to avoid in your history papers.

Prefer the active voice. As noted in Chapter 1, historians are like detectives; they try to answer questions like *Who? What? Where?* and *When?* Using the passive voice can obscure this information. Consider the following excerpt from a student essay:

PASSIVE VOICE

In 1521, Tenochtitlan was invaded and the Aztecs were defeated.

Because he uses the passive voice here, the writer omits a vital piece of information: *who* invaded Tenochtitlan and defeated the Aztecs?

In addition, the passive voice sometimes hides fuzzy thinking and allows writers to be vague about the connections between people, events, and ideas. Note what happens, for instance, when the writer of the previous example uses the active voice:

ACTIVE VOICE

In 1521, the Spanish conquistador Hernán Cortés and his army, supported by native allies like the Tlaxcalans, lay siege to the city of Tenochtitlan. Three months later, the hardships of the siege and the devastation caused by a smallpox epidemic forced the Aztec ruler, Cuauhtemoc, to surrender.

Because he is using the active voice here, the writer must identify the actors (Cortés, his army, and his native allies). Moreover, using the active voice also forces him to consider the complexity of the historical reality: The "invasion" of Tenochtitlan was really a three-month siege, and the defeat of the Aztecs was the result of the combined efforts of Cortés's army and native allies, the devastating effects of a long siege, and the impact of a new and virulent disease. Using the active voice thus requires the writer to provide more—and more specific—information.

In addition, the passive voice makes the writer sound hesitant. For example, the expression "it can be argued that" suggests that the writer is unwilling to take responsibility for his or her arguments. If your evidence leads you to a certain conclusion, state it clearly. Similarly, the expression "it has been argued that" can confuse readers: Who has made this argument? How many people and in what context? Readers must have this information to evaluate the argument. Moreover, use of the passive voice can result in plagiarism. If one or more persons have argued a particular point, you should identify them in the text and provide a citation.

Use the passive voice in special situations.   While historians almost always prefer the active voice, there are some special circumstances in which the passive voice is useful. Consider the following description of the Holocaust (verbs in the passive voice have been italicized):

Hitler engaged in the ruthless oppression and systematic murder of the Jewish people. In 1933, Jews *were forbidden* to hold public office; by 1935, they *were deprived* of citizenship. In all, over six million Jews *were killed* as part of Hitler's "final solution."

In this passage, the writer wants to draw the reader's attention to the recipients of the action—the six million Jews killed in the Holocaust. The persons acted on are more important than the actor. The passive voice, which focuses attention on the victims, is therefore appropriate. The passive voice, then, can be effective, but it should be used only occasionally and for a specific reason.

4g-4 Knowing when to use the pronouns *I, me,* and *you*

Although you may occasionally see the pronouns *I, me,* and *you* in history books and journal articles, most professional historians use these pronouns sparingly, or not at all, and most history instructors prefer students to avoid them whenever possible. However, a number of professors find their use not only acceptable but actually preferable to more labored constructions like "this evidence leads one to conclude that." Since the conventions governing the use of personal pronouns are in flux, it is best to consult your instructor about his or her preference. In any case, it is important to be consistent; if you use personal pronouns in the first paragraph ("My argument is based on the evidence of several primary sources"), don't switch to an impersonal construction in the second ("On the basis of the evidence, one might argue that . . .").

5

Writing a Research Paper

Chapter 4 introduced you to the basic elements of writing a history essay: developing a thesis, using evidence to construct an argument, organizing your material effectively, and writing clearly. Like a short essay, a research paper usually takes the form of an argument in support of a thesis based on evidence from sources. It is different from a short essay, however, in several ways. First, a research paper is more substantial, usually at least fifteen pages and often much longer. More important, a research paper requires that you go beyond the assigned readings for the course and engage in a significant amount of independent work.

Your instructor might assign a specific research topic, or the choice might be left entirely up to you. Most often, you will be given some choice within a general area. The syllabus for a course with a research paper might, for example, include a statement like this in its list of course requirements:

> Research paper on any topic covered in the course, chosen in consultation with me. This paper should be 15–18 pages and is worth 40% of your final grade.

You may find such assignments intimidating and secretly yearn for an assigned subject; it often seems easier to write about a topic that holds no interest for you than to face the task of defining your own area of investigation. However, when you choose your own research topic, you are actually doing the same work that a professional historian does: conducting research in order to answer the questions *you* have posed about a subject that *you* find compelling or problematic and then writing a paper that allows *you* to enter into a conversation with other scholars who are interested in similar questions and problems. The research paper, then, is both challenging and enormously exciting. It allows you, while still a student, to undertake original research and perhaps even discover something new. This, rather than its length, is what truly distinguishes the research project from other writing assignments.

Writing a research paper is an extremely complex activity; it does not proceed in a simple linear fashion, step by step. For the sake of clarity, this chapter divides the process of writing a research paper into the following stages: choosing a topic and focusing on a research question that you will answer in your paper, developing a research plan and a working thesis, conducting research, taking effective notes, writing an outline, and revising your paper. You should keep in mind, however, that real research involves a constant interaction of thinking, reading, and writing, and that the processes outlined in these sections will intersect and overlap.

5a Moving from topic to research question

Deciding what topic to write about can seem overwhelming; out of an apparently infinite range of possibilities, how do you choose? The process is more manageable if you break it down into its component parts: choosing a broad subject that interests you, narrowing your focus to a topic that you will be able to write about in the time and space allotted, deciding what you want to know about that topic, and, finally, formulating the research question you want to answer in your paper.

5a-1 Choosing a topic

Since a research paper represents a significant investment of time and effort, you will produce your best work if you choose a topic that can sustain your interest over the course of an entire semester.

Start with the texts assigned for your class and find a general area that appeals to you. This might be a relatively

wide-ranging subject, like "slavery and the Civil War."
Obviously, this is much too broad—you will not be able
to write an effective essay on this subject within the length
of a typical research paper—and you will need to narrow
your focus. However, you will not know what problems,
issues, and questions exist within the larger framework of
the subject in which you are interested until you familiarize yourself with the research done by other scholars.

Narrowing a broad subject to a feasible topic for a
research paper always begins with reading. You might
start with a book assigned for your class. In addition, you
might want to consult dictionaries, encyclopedias, and
other general resources to get some background information about your subject. Such sources should never be
your main sources of information for research papers at
the college level, but reputable encyclopedias can provide
useful background to get you started. (See Appendix B
for a list of some reliable dictionaries, encyclopedias, and
other resources in history.)

You should also determine what sources are available
to you, either in your own college or university library,
through interlibrary or consortium loans, or on the Internet. For example, you might decide that it would be interesting to examine the views of artisans during the French
Revolution, but if you cannot obtain enough sources of
information on this subject, this will not be a workable
topic. Similarly, you should find out whether the sources
for the topic in which you are interested are written in a
language that you can read fluently. You might find that
there are extensive collections of sources on artisans in
revolutionary France—written in French. In this case, is
your command of the language sufficient for the research
you hope to pursue?

5a-2 Focusing on a research question

As you do your preliminary reading, you should be looking for a particular aspect of the topic that you want to
explore further. For example, if your topic is "slavery and
the Civil War," you might be particularly interested in the
role of abolitionists in the war, in the events and ideas
that led up to the Emancipation Proclamation, or perhaps in what slaves thought about the war. Then, having
identified what you hope to learn, you should be able to

state your topic as a *single question* that can be answered as a result of your research. Ultimately, the answer to your research question will take the form of a *thesis*, the main argument of your paper. (For more on thesis statements, see 4c.) The following are some tips for asking good research questions:

- **Avoid questions that elicit simple description.** Focusing on a question such as "What was the Compromise of 1850?" or "What happened during the Battle of Bull Run?" can result in a paper that is merely a list of facts or a narrative reporting "what happened next," neither of which is a satisfactory research paper.

- **Avoid yes/no questions.** Your research question should not be one that would generate a simple yes or no answer. Once you have answered the question "Did free blacks play a role in the Union army?" where would you go from there?

- **Avoid questions that are too broad.** You will not be able to answer the question "What role did freed slaves play in the Civil War?" in a twelve- to fifteen-page paper.

- **Avoid leading or rhetorical questions.** Don't make unwarranted assumptions or presume a particular answer. The question "Why were Northern states more racially integrated than Southern states in the 1800s?" presumes that the North was, in fact, more egalitarian than the South. Such a question might lead you to collect only evidence that supported your assumption while ignoring evidence to the contrary.

- **Avoid speculative questions.** The question "What would have happened if the South had won the Civil War?" might provoke some interesting speculations, but it is *not* a question that could be answered by historical research. Instead, ask questions that will allow you to develop an argument based on evidence.

Since your goal is to create a thesis—and a paper—that takes a stand on a particular issue, you should ask *a meaningful historical question that calls for analysis and interpretation, and that might elicit some debate.* You might, for instance, look at a particular Union regiment and try to answer the question "How did white Union officers' assumptions about race affect the way they treated black soldiers under their command?" Such a question would allow you to enter a scholarly debate by formulating your own research-based opinion.

5b Developing a research plan and a working thesis

Section 5a hinted at the effort you will need to put into gathering, reading, and evaluating texts as you move from selecting and narrowing your topic to developing a research question. Obviously, a research paper is a serious scholarly endeavor; it cannot be done effectively at the last minute. Some professors break the research process into phases for you. You might be asked to produce a written topic proposal, an annotated bibliography, an outline, and a rough draft of your paper as separate graded assignments. In this case, much of the time-management difficulties involved in the production of a research paper will have been done for you. More often, you will need to develop a research plan for yourself.

In planning your research strategy, you should consider what information you will need at each stage of the process, what sources you will need to consult in order to acquire that information, where you can find those sources, and how much time you will need to allow for research. Your research plan should reflect the subject you have chosen. For example, if the subject on which you are writing is obscure, locating sources may take significantly more time than if you are writing about a relatively well-known subject. In the first case, you would probably need to allocate more time to evaluating primary sources that have not been well studied, while in the second instance, you would need more time to read and evaluate what other scholars have said. In either case, you would need to allow enough time to find and gather the materials needed; develop a working bibliography; read, evaluate, and take notes on your sources; and formulate a working thesis.

It is always safest to anticipate problems in gathering your sources: Other people may have borrowed the books you want, or you may have to travel to other libraries or archives to use their collections. If you are interested in a topic for which your own library has only limited sources, you might be able to borrow books from other colleges and universities on interlibrary loan, but processing those loans requires time, so plan accordingly.

5b-1 Gathering and managing sources

Once you have decided on a topic, you should begin to gather sources for your paper. A good research paper contains references to a variety of sources, so you will need to develop a strategy for finding useful sources; you will also need to find ways to keep track of and synthesize the material they contain. Section 5c contains in-depth advice on conducting research, but the following preliminary tips provide an overview of how to begin gathering and working with your sources efficiently and intelligently.

Identify both primary and secondary sources. For most research papers, you will need to consult primary sources (letters, diaries, original documents, and so on) from the period you are studying. You will also need to consult secondary sources to become familiar with the ways in which other historians have interpreted this material. Your secondary sources should reflect a balance of materials. While books are valuable sources, you should not confine your research to books; important recent research is often found in scholarly journal articles. You will probably find both primary and secondary sources on the Internet; however, you should note that Internet sources alone are not sufficient for a research paper. In any case, you should evaluate the usefulness and reliability of your sources as you read, using the criteria set out in Chapter 2. Finally, as you begin to gather sources, always keep your research question in mind. If you allow yourself to be sidetracked by fascinating material that is not related to your research question, your paper will lose its focus and you may have trouble making your deadline.

Use nonwritten materials where appropriate. Although much of the work you do in an undergraduate history course will depend on the reading and interpretation of written sources, historians also use a wide variety of nonwritten sources in their work. The following types of nonwritten materials may be useful to you in researching and writing your paper:

- **Maps** are especially useful for explaining geographical relationships, such as the movements of troops during a battle or the changes in the national boundaries of a particular area over time.

- **Graphs and charts** are useful for illustrating statistical information, such as rates of marriages, births, or deaths and changes in per capita income over a period of time.

- **Photographs, cartoons, and other illustrations** may provide evidence that supports or contradicts the written sources, or may provide a unique perspective on events.

- **Oral history sources**, such as interviews, can be useful for information about events that have occurred within living memory, such as the Vietnam War. In addition, some research organizations, such as the United States Holocaust Memorial Museum (http://www.ushmm.org/research/collections/oral history/), archive oral history sources online. Historians have developed special methodologies for conducting oral history, so you should seek your professor's advice before engaging in this type of research.

- **Diagrams**, such as a cross-section of the Great Pyramid, can help the reader understand how parts are related to a larger whole. (For information on how to evaluate nonwritten sources, see the Tips for Writers box on pp. 12–13.)

Keep a working bibliography.   As you gather sources for your research, you should keep a working bibliography in which you record complete bibliographic information for every item you have examined. (See 7c-2 for a description of the elements that constitute complete bibliographic information.) Nothing is more frustrating than to return all your books to the library only to discover that you are missing authors' names, dates of publication, or other information you will need for your bibliography. You should also record complete bibliographical information for any nonwritten sources you examine or cite. If you have not written many academic papers, you may find it difficult to remember all of the elements that should be included in a bibliographic entry; therefore, while doing your research, you may want to keep this guide handy. Or you may find it useful to list the information you need to record on an index card that you can carry with you.

Note: Do not make generating a bibliography an end in itself. You still need to read the books and articles you have found! Your final bibliography should include only the materials you have read and found useful in writing your paper.

5b-2 Developing a working thesis

In a research paper, where you pose your own research question and conduct significant independent work, the role of the thesis is particularly crucial. (See 4c for details on how to write an effective thesis.) All of the preliminary reading that you do for your research paper and the writing that attends that reading (listing questions, taking notes, jotting down ideas, and so on) is intended to stimulate and clarify your thinking. The result of all of this thinking and reading and writing is the generation of a *working thesis*: a single sentence in which you suggest a *tentative* answer to your research question. From this point on, your research process should center on this working thesis. All of the sources you plan to include in your paper should provide evidence to support it or help you respond to arguments that might be raised against it.

Keep in mind, however, that the thesis at this stage in the production of a research paper is only a *working* thesis. As you gather, read, and evaluate texts, organize your notes, develop ideas about your topic, and begin to write the paper itself, it is important to remain flexible. Your working thesis should lead to additional reading, and the evidence you uncover in the course of that reading must always lead you to test your thesis—does it still hold up as you find out new information or encounter new interpretations? Willingness to modify a thesis in response to research is the hallmark of a good historian.

5c Conducting research

In order to explore the possible answers to your research question, you will need to identify and evaluate a substantial number of primary and secondary sources of various types. Moreover, once you have developed a working thesis, you will need to conduct even more research to refine and test it. But how do you go about finding the sources you will need to write an effective research paper? This section provides some suggestions for how to use print and electronic research tools to locate reliable sources from among the wealth of materials available to you.

5c-1 Consulting human resources

You might have so much experience with the Internet that your first instinct is to begin a research project by going online. However, you will save a great deal of time and effort if you begin by consulting two very important human resources.

Begin by consulting your professor. Although a research paper may seem daunting to you, remember that your professor has had a great deal of experience in conducting research and writing papers and is intimately familiar with the research produced by other historians. Take advantage of office hours, chat rooms, course-based Web sites, and other forums for consulting your professor. He or she will be delighted by your interest and will be happy to point you in a number of potentially fruitful directions. Ask your professor to recommend books and articles on your topic, and use them at the outset of your research. Your professor can also direct you to the most important scholarly journals in the field you are researching. And, of course, you should always consult your professor if you have any questions about what kinds of sources are required or allowed. For example, you might want to ask which Internet sources are acceptable, if any, and whether field research such as oral history is allowed or encouraged.

Consult a reference librarian. Reference librarians are invaluable resources that are too often overlooked. They are extremely helpful in tracking down important print and electronic journals, bibliographies, book reviews, and other research tools. Reference librarians can also teach you how to search your university's online catalog and how to use the databases to which your university subscribes.

5c-2 Locating primary sources

Primary sources are the essential materials with which historians work, and you will find primary sources in both print and electronic formats. Book-length sources, like novels, chronicles, and memoirs, are available in print, either in their original form or in editions and translations. (See Chapter 2 for advice on how to evaluate translations and editions of primary sources.) Many are also available as e-texts (whole books posted online). You may be able to examine original primary sources like letters, diaries, wills, or photographs directly at an archive; more commonly, you will be using print or digitized document collections that have been organized for you by an editor. You might also find oral history archives, such as the Library of Congress's *Veterans History Project* (http://www.loc.gov/vets/) online. In addition, you can find government documents and newspapers, both current and archived, from around the world on the Internet. Specialized primary source collections for virtually every historical period worldwide can also be found online. To locate these collections, you may want to begin with a general history Web site like *Academic Info History Gateway* (http://www.academicinfo.net/hist.html) or a reference book like Dennis Trinkle and Scott Merriman's *The History Highway: A 21st Century Guide to Internet Resources.* Several other valuable collections of primary sources on the Web are included in Appendix B and in the appendices of the Internet guides listed in Appendix A.

Note: As you look for primary sources on the Internet, keep in mind that to abide by copyright laws, some Web sites, particularly those dealing with older materials, may post editions or translations of sources that are in the public domain. (A reputable Web site will inform you if this is the case.) Editions that are in the public domain were made so long ago that they are no longer covered by copyright restrictions. In such cases, the Internet is still an extremely useful tool for making you aware of the wide variety of sources that are available, but once you find a source you intend to use, you will probably want to look elsewhere for the most recent printed edition or translation. Moreover, many primary and secondary sources are not yet available on the Internet. Students who rely solely on electronic media will miss many fundamental and indispensable sources. It is vital, therefore, that you consult both electronic *and* print sources in your research.

5c-3 Using the library's online catalog

After consulting your professor and a research librarian, you should start your own search for sources in your university's library. Begin by acquainting yourself with the library's layout. Locate the stacks and reference room; find out if your library has microfilm or microfiche materials; determine if there is a rare book room. Many universities also have archives that you might want to access for special projects. Next, familiarize yourself with your library's online catalog. Each library's home page is unique; however, they all typically direct students to the resources available in their own library, and most include links to a variety of electronic sources, including databases, reference sources, journals, subscription-only services, and e-texts. Most library home pages also provide access to the Internet and links to other college and university libraries.

Sources available in a university library usually include books, scholarly journals, audio and/or video recordings, CD-ROMs, and microform/microfilm materials such as back issues of newspapers. You can usually search the library's online catalog by author, title, subject, or keyword.

If your professor has recommended a specific book, searching by title or author is simple and efficient. You can then find other books of interest by browsing the shelves in the area where your book is housed, since books on the same topic are grouped together. Also consult the bibliographies and notes of any useful books you find; these will lead you to other primary and secondary sources of interest.

If you don't have a particular book in mind, you can conduct a subject or keyword search. Keep in mind, however, that a subject search reflects the formal Library of Congress subject listings, which may not always be obvious. It is usually best to try a keyword search, using as many keywords as you can think of that might lead you to materials on your topic. For example, you might look for materials on the medieval plague by entering *bubonic plague*, *Black Death*, and *Black Plague*, each of which would yield slightly different results. You can search the online catalog most effectively by conducting an advanced or guided keyword search that allows you to include or exclude specific terms in your search parameters. For example, if you wanted to examine the plague in continental Europe in the fourteenth century, you could limit your search to *Black Death* AND *14th century* NOT *England*. Your online catalog will provide instructions for conducting a guided keyword search, and the time you invest in learning how to do this will make your search much more efficient.

Unless you attend a major research university, you might want to expand your search to other institutions' holdings. Often, your library's home page will include links to local colleges and universities whose catalogs you can also search online. If you find materials of interest, you can usually order them through interlibrary loan; increasingly, articles can be sent electronically to your library or even directly to your own e-mail address. Finally, your library's home page may include a link to e-texts. Clearly, then, you can use the online catalog of your university's library to open up a broad research base.

5c-4 Using print and electronic reference sources

As noted in 5a, you may want to consult a variety of print and electronic reference sources at the beginning of your research process. Useful sources include encyclopedias, both general (such as *Encyclopaedia Britannica*) and specialized (such as *The Encyclopedia of the Vietnam War*); topical and biographical dictionaries (such as *The Historical Dictionary of the Elizabethan World* or *The New Dictionary of National Biography*); chronologies; and atlases. Keep in mind that you should look for both print and electronic sources. You will find print sources in your library's reference room. The library's home page will typically provide links to reliable online reference sources as well, some of which are available only by subscription and may therefore be accessed at library terminals only. Sometimes, these sources may be organized for you by subject. For example, your library may provide a research guide for history that lists links to electronic resources of interest to historians. Several important print and online reference works are listed in Appendix B.

Note: Some free encyclopedias are available online, but they are not all equally reliable. As noted in 2b-3, the popular online encyclopedia *Wikipedia* is a public forum that allows any reader to add or edit entries. Consequently, the entries may be inaccurate or biased, and many instructors will not accept *Wikipedia* as a reference in your paper. Before you use an Internet reference source, make sure you know who has written the entries and what organization sponsors the Web site. Better still, use the links on your library's home page to guide you to appropriate online reference sources.

5c-5 Using print and electronic periodical databases

Recently published journal articles not only represent the most scholarly and up-to-date work on the topic in which you are interested, but they frequently contain an overview of the academic work on the subject and provide references to other important books and articles. To find the most relevant articles for your topic, you will need to use both print and electronic bibliographies, indexes, and periodical databases.

Many library reference rooms contain comprehensive print indexes, such as *Humanities Index* (also available electronically), which list important secondary sources and are arranged by subject matter for ease of browsing. Print indexes contain all the bibliographic information needed to track down an article; some indexes, such as *Historical Abstracts*, also contain abstracts, which briefly summarize the contents of the articles listed. Most likely, your school library also subscribes to dozens of electronic databases, such as *Periodicals Index Online*, which you can access through a research gateway from your school's Web site (at some schools, access is restricted to library terminals only). Generally speaking, electronic databases are easier to search than print indexes, and in some cases they provide full-text access to the articles listed. In addition, many electronic databases may be more readily available than print indexes; check with your school's reference librarian for the best place to begin searching for scholarly articles in your subject area. The Tips for Writers box on page 79 displays a list of some of the most useful electronic databases for history students and what they offer; Appendix B provides a more comprehensive list of resources for researching in history.

5c-6 Finding Internet sources

Used with care and with a critical eye, the Internet can be an invaluable supplement to your research, providing access to a wide variety of sources that would otherwise be unavailable. As you move outside your library's electronic

Tips for Writers
Electronic Databases

Database name	Area of specialty	Print version available	Full-text archives*	Dates
America: History and Life	American and Canadian history and culture	Yes	Some	1964–present
Historical Abstracts	World history from 1450; excludes U.S. and Canada	Yes	Some	1954–present
Humanities Index	Humanities (including history)	Yes	Some	1984–present
Journal Storage Project (JSTOR)	Scholarly journals dating back to 1600s	No	Yes	1600s–within last 5 years
Periodicals Index Online	Scholarly journals dating back to 1600s	Yes	Some	1600s–present
Project Muse	Scholarly journal articles posted online	No	Yes	1990s–present
Social Sciences Citation Index	Social sciences (including history)	Yes	Some	1956–present

*Note: In many cases, databases will attempt to provide a link to the full text of an article, even if the article isn't included in the database's own archives. Check with your reference librarian to find out what is available.

environment onto the Internet, however, make sure to use caution. Be aware that many Web sites are useless for serious research; in fact, many instructors either forbid

Internet sources outright or require that you get their permission before using them in a paper. If your instructor does allow Internet sources, be sure your search stays on the right track by keeping the following advice in mind.

Begin by browsing links related to your topic from a source that you can trust. Your instructor may have useful links posted on his or her Web site, and your school library may keep an updated collection of links organized by discipline. You can also refer to the many sites listed in Appendix B of this text. In addition, if you come across a site that appears to be a reputable source on a particular topic, you may find that its links are also worth checking out.

In general, you will want to avoid doing simple key-word searches on search engines such as Yahoo! and Google because the results will be overwhelming and the reliability of the links will be dubious. These search engines do, however, provide advanced search pages and other specialized areas, such as Yahoo!'s directory and Google's Scholar, that can help you fine-tune your search to return only the most relevant and reputable sites. Using the advanced search features, for example, you can limit your search results to education (.edu) or government (.gov) sites only, or retrieve only those sites that have been recently updated. When you find a useful source that you might want to access again later, bookmark it or, if you are working from a public computer, e-mail yourself a link or jot down the URL.

Note: Always evaluate the reliability of any Web site you plan to use by following the criteria outlined in 2b-3.

5c-7 Distinguishing among electronic sources

Since many types of sources can be accessed electronically, you may sometimes find yourself wondering where exactly your source has come from and how reliable it is. Is it from an electronic database? An online journal? A government Web site? When trying to make these important distinctions, keep the following points in mind.

Databases. Databases store digitized versions of materials that usually have print equivalents. (Some databases that are particularly useful for history students are listed in the

Tips for Writers box on p. 79.) Although a database may contain a wide variety of sources, including popular titles such as *Newsweek* and *American Heritage,* you can generally tailor your search to include only scholarly sources such as academic journals. Since your tuition dollars pay for these subscriptions, in most cases you will need to identify yourself as a student to access these valuable storehouses of information. Note that the database will look like any other Web site, usually with a .com extension, but you won't see any advertisements or links to external sites.

Web sites for periodicals.   Many print periodicals—popular magazines, scholarly journals, newspapers—maintain companion Web sites. These Web sites are primarily for advertising and subscription purposes, and they are of limited use to researchers. You will likely be able to access the current edition, and perhaps some of the more recent articles, but you will probably not be able to download older full-text articles without paying a fee.

Online-only journals have no print counterparts. To determine whether an online-only publication is credible—whether it is affiliated with an academic institution and if the articles are peer-reviewed—you should always check the "About" link. Several reputable online-only journals are listed in Appendix B.

Broadcast news Web sites.   Most major news outlets—NBC, Fox, NPR, CNN—have Web sites that archive their news stories. Yahoo! News provides news in an Internet-only format.

Government Web sites.   Government agencies typically provide useful information online for public use, including census and immigration data, legislative records, economic statistics, and historical documents. The URLs for these sites typically contain the extension *.gov* or, for state governments, *.us* plus a state abbreviation such as *.ma.*

Other Web sites.   Countless organizations, schools, museums, foundations, and so on have Web sites to store and display their collections, which are of tremendous value to researchers. Web sites from sources other than these (and the ones listed above), however, are probably either commercial—existing primarily to sell a product or collect advertising revenue—or personal. Commercial and personal sites are the two most unreliable types of online sources because they are generally biased and/or not scholarly. In general, avoid commercial or personal sites; if you do wish to use them, you should ask your instructor first and take extra precautions when evaluating them (see 2b-3).

5d   Taking effective research notes

Your final paper will only be as good as the notes you take. There is no right or wrong way to take notes for a research paper. Many people favor index cards that can be arranged and rearranged easily. Others prefer to use notebooks or legal pads. Some type notes directly into an electronic file. Whatever method you use, there are several things you can do to make your note taking more effective.

Write as you read.   As explained in section 3a, reading and writing are interactive processes. The writing you do while reading can take many different forms. If you own some of the books you are using for your paper, or if you have made photocopies of some of the important materials you will be using, you might want to write directly on the text, underlining important points and making comments in the margins. Develop your own code for marginal notation so that you will be able to identify arguments that you find questionable, insights that you find important, or words that you need to define. (For further suggestions on writing as you read, see the Tips for Writers box on p. 23.) You should also write notes to yourself about any ideas, insights, or questions that occur to you as you read. This writing will help you clarify your thoughts about what you are reading and provide direction for your research.

Always record complete bibliographic information for your sources.   It is absolutely essential that you be able to identify the source of any facts, ideas, visuals, or quotations that you derive from your research, and that you clearly differentiate the ideas of others from your own. Careful note taking will save you lots of time tracking down quotations and will ensure that you do not plagiarize inadvertently.

Take most of your notes in the form of summaries. If you take notes word for word from your source, you are simply acting as a human photocopier. Your goal should be to digest the information presented in your sources and make it your own. It is much more useful to read carefully and thoughtfully, close the book, and summarize in your own words the section you have read. Then compare your summary with the original, noting any important points that you missed or anything that you misunderstood. At this point, you should also check carefully to make sure that you have not inadvertently taken any words or phrases directly from the original text. This type of note taking will not only ensure that you really understand the material but also help you avoid plagiarism.

Copy quotations accurately. If you do decide to quote directly from a source, make sure you copy the words and punctuation exactly, and always use quotation marks so that you will know it is a direct quote when you return to your notes. Do not try to improve the wording of the original or correct the spelling or grammar. You may, however, alert your readers to an error in spelling or grammar by recording the error as it appears in the source and then noting the mistake by adding the Latin word *sic* (meaning "thus") in brackets: "Do not correct mispelled [*sic*] words." (For advice on using and citing quotations, see Chapter 7.)

Avoid the misconception that "to photocopy is to know." Photocopying material on your topic is no substitute for reading and understanding it. Photocopying doesn't save time; in fact, unless you are photocopying important sources so that you can annotate them, it is often a waste of both time and money. Eventually, you will have to read and interpret the photocopied material, and when you do, you may notice that you have copied irrelevant material and missed important information.

5e Making an outline

Note taking, however precise and clear, is not an end in itself. The notes you take should be directed toward providing the information you will need to refine and support your working thesis as you attempt to answer your research question. If you have taken careful notes while conducting research, you will be able to organize them into an outline in which you sketch out the body of your paper.

The most important function of an outline is to provide a guide that identifies the points you wish to cover and the order in which you plan to cover them. A good outline will help you present the evidence that supports your thesis as a convincing argument. Some students have been trained to write formal outlines with roman numerals and various subheadings. If this method works for you, by all means use it. Many students find formal outlines too constraining and prefer instead to write a less formal outline. You might begin an informal outline by writing down the main points you want to discuss. These will form the topic sentences of paragraphs. Underneath each main point, list the evidence that supports it. Outlining your paper in this way will reveal any points that require additional evidence. It will also help ensure that your evidence is organized logically and that each idea is connected to those that precede and follow it.

Finally, remember that an outline is a tool. As you continue to think and write about your subject, you may discover new material or change your mind about the significance of the material you have examined. You may even change your thesis (which is why your thesis at this stage is still a working thesis rather than a final one). When this happens, you must be willing to revise your outline too.

If you have taken careful and thorough notes and organized them effectively in an outline, what originally seemed to be a daunting task will become much more manageable. The advice in Chapter 4 on following the conventions of writing history papers will provide guidance as you write the first draft of your research paper.

5f   Revising and editing your paper

As you revise, think about whether you have organized your argument in the most effective manner. Also determine whether you have presented enough evidence to support your thesis. You may even decide at this stage that you need to conduct additional research; this is one way in which revising a research paper differs from revising a short essay. Most important, you should reexamine your thesis in light of the evidence you have provided, evaluate the validity of that thesis, and modify or change it completely if necessary. (For more advice on revising your paper, see 4f.) Finally, once your revision is complete, you will need to edit your paper to correct grammatical and typographical errors. (Additional advice on word choice and grammar can be found in 4g.)

A research paper is a complex project. It is unrealistic to expect that one or two drafts will be sufficient to do justice to it. As you plan your research, make sure you leave yourself sufficient time to revise and edit thoroughly. Obviously, a research paper represents a significant commitment of time, effort, and intellect. Nonetheless, the rewards are equally great, for it is in the research paper that you can experience the pleasures of truly original interpretation and discovery.

6

Plagiarism

WHAT IT IS AND HOW TO AVOID IT

Plagiarism is the act of taking the words, ideas, or research of another person and putting them forward without citation as if they were your own. It is intellectual theft and a clear violation of the code of ethics and behavior that most academic institutions have established to regulate the scholastic conduct of their members. Most colleges and universities have their own policies that define plagiarism and establish guidelines for dealing with plagiarism cases and punishing offenders, but the penalties for plagiarism are usually severe, ranging from an automatic F in the course to temporary suspension or even permanent expulsion from the school. Plagiarism, in short, is considered a very serious academic offense.

If we look simply at the dictionary definition, it would seem that acts of plagiarism are readily identifiable. And, indeed, some instances of plagiarism are obvious: deliberately copying lengthy passages from a book or journal article, submitting an essay written by a classmate as your own, or purchasing or downloading whole papers and submitting them under your own name. However, although some students unfortunately make a conscious decision to plagiarize, many more do so inadvertently. This is because, unlike the instances cited above, some situations in which you might use the words or ideas of another may seem murkier. Because of its seriousness, it is essential that you know exactly what kinds of acts constitute plagiarism. This chapter will clarify the concept and give you some advice on how to avoid plagiarism.

6a What is plagiarism?

Read the following scenarios. Which of these would be considered plagiarism?

- A student borrows a friend's essay to get some ideas for his own paper. With his friend's permission, he copies portions of it, taking care, however, to cite all the sources his friend included in the original.
- A student finds useful information on a Web site that is not under copyright. She downloads and incorporates sections of this Web site into her paper, but does not cite it since it is in the public domain.
- A student derives some key ideas for his paper from a book. Since he doesn't quote anything directly from this book, he doesn't provide any footnotes. He does, however, include the book in his bibliography.
- A student modifies the original text by changing some words, leaving out an example, and rearranging the order of the material. Since she is not using the exact words of the original, she does not include a footnote.

The answer is that *all four* of these scenarios illustrate examples of plagiarism. In the first instance, the issue is not whether the student has permission from his friend to use his or her work. As long as the student is submitting work done by another as his own, it is plagiarism. Citing the sources that his friend has used does not mitigate the charge of plagiarism. In the second example, the fact that the student has used material that is not protected by copyright is irrelevant. She is guilty of plagiarism because she has submitted the words of another as her own. The third instance illustrates that the definition of plagiarism encompasses the use not only of someone else's words but also of his or her ideas; you must always acknowledge the source of your ideas in a footnote or endnote, even if you specifically include the text in your bibliography. Finally, in the fourth example, changing some of the words, reorganizing the material, or leaving out some phrases does not constitute a genuine paraphrase; moreover, even an effective paraphrase requires a footnote.

As a history student you are part of a community of scholars; when you write history papers, you become part of the intellectual conversation of that community. The published words and ideas of other historians are there to be used—but as a matter of intellectual honesty, you are bound to acknowledge their contributions to your own thought.

6b   Avoiding plagiarism

Most unintentional plagiarism can be traced to three sources: confusion about when and how to cite sources, uncertainty about how to paraphrase, and carelessness in taking notes and downloading Internet materials.

6b-1   Citing sources to avoid plagiarism

When you derive facts and ideas from other writers' work, you must cite the sources of your information. Most students are aware that they must cite the sources of direct quotations. However, students sometimes assume, erroneously, that direct quotations are the *only* things they need to cite. In fact, borrowing ideas from other writers without documenting them is a form of plagiarism every bit as serious as taking their words. Therefore, you must provide citations for *all* information derived from another source, *even if you have summarized or paraphrased the information*. Furthermore, you must also cite your sources when you use other writers' *interpretations* of a historical event or text. In short, you should remember that anytime you use information derived from another person's work, build on another writer's ideas, or adopt someone else's interpretation, you must acknowledge your source. This enables your readers to distinguish between your ideas and those of others.

The only exception is that you do not need to provide citations for information that is common knowledge. *Common knowledge* is generally defined as well-known facts that can be found in multiple reference works and are not subject to debate. For example, you might have learned from a particular book that the Civil War spanned the years 1861 to 1865, but you do not have to cite the book when you include this fact in your paper. You could have obtained the time span of the Civil War from any number of sources because it is common knowledge. The more you read about your subject, the easier it will be for you to distinguish common knowledge from information that needs a citation. When in doubt, however, it is better to be safe and cite the source. (For additional information on quoting and citing sources, including documentation models, see Chapter 7.)

Note: One practice that will help you avoid plagiarism is to keep all of your research notes and rough drafts in separate files. Then, as you prepare your final draft, you will be able to check your notes if you are uncertain about whether a particular phrase is a direct quote or a paraphrase, or where an idea or quotation came from. (See 5d for more on careful note taking.)

6b-2 Paraphrasing to avoid plagiarism

Most students know that copying a passage word for word from a source is plagiarism. However, many are unsure about how to paraphrase. Consider, for example, this passage from a recent book on the history of food and the unacceptable student paraphrase that follows:

ORIGINAL PASSAGE

The slave trade destroyed families, killed spiritual expression, and undermined the material world of transplanted Africans. This cultural holocaust was comprehensive, ruinous, and unrelenting. Remarkably, however, slaves refused to acquiesce to the brutality completely. They refused to sacrifice their basic sense of humanity. In fact, faced with such adversity, West Indian slaves discovered unique ways to forge a culture that blended their African heritage with New World conditions, however desperate those conditions may have been. Cast adrift in a sea of violence and greed, they sought, against all odds, to cling to at least a semblance of their inherited traditions. The most notable of these traditions was culinary.[1]

UNACCEPTABLE PARAPHRASE

Slavery ruined families, destroyed religious expression, and damaged the material world of the Africans who were brought to the West Indies. This cultural destruction was complete and unending. Amazingly, however, slaves didn't give in. They refused to sacrifice their basic sense of being human. In fact, faced with such hardships, they found unique ways to make a new culture that brought together their African heritage with conditions in the New World. In spite of violence and greed, they tried to hold on to their inherited traditions. The most notable of these traditions was food.

1. James E. McWilliams, *A Revolution in Eating: How the Quest for Food Shaped America* (New York: Columbia University Press, 2005), 29–30.

In this example, the writer's attempt at paraphrase results in plagiarism, *despite the fact* that the second text is not an exact copy of the original. First, the writer has not acknowledged the source of his information; even though there is no direct quotation, a citation is required. Second, this paragraph would be considered plagiarism *even if* the writer acknowledged the source of the material by including a citation. The writer has used a thesaurus to find synonyms for several words—*destroyed* has become *ruined*, *comprehensive* has been replaced by *complete*, and *hardships* has been substituted for *adversity*. In addition, several words or phrases in the original have been left out in the second version, and the word order has occasionally been rearranged. Nevertheless, these changes are merely editorial. The new paragraph is not significantly different from the original in either form or substance; it is simply too close to the original to be considered the work of the student.

In a genuine paraphrase, the writer has thought about what the source says and absorbed it. Once the writer understands the content of the source, he can restate it in an entirely original way that reflects his own wording and style. Consider, for example, this paraphrase:

ACCEPTABLE PARAPHRASE

According to historian James McWilliams, the slave trade had a dev-astating effect on the family structure, religious practices, and way of life of the Africans who were brought to the West Indies. Despite the incredible hardships they endured, however, these men and women managed to adapt elements of their traditional practices to the new, and often terrible, circumstances of their lives as enslaved people. In this process of building a new cultural identity, McWilliams argues, food played a central role.[2]

---

2. James E. McWilliams, *A Revolution in Eating: How the Quest for Food Shaped America* (New York: Columbia University Press, 2005), 29–30.

This paraphrase is more successful; the writer has assimilated the content of the source and expressed it in his own words, relaying to the reader his understanding of what McWilliams said. You should also note that the writer has indicated the source of his information by using signal phrases such as "according to historian James McWilliams" and "McWilliams argues." Finally, even though the writer has not used any direct quotations, and has mentioned his source by name in the text, he has also provided a footnote indicating the exact source of his information. Without this citation, this paraphrase would be considered plagiarism. (You can find detailed information about how to cite sources in Chapter 7.)

You will save time if you paraphrase as you take notes. However, if you attempt to paraphrase with the original source open in front of you, you are courting disaster. To write a genuine paraphrase, you should close the book and summarize in your own words what you have read. Then, go back and check the original source to make sure that you have not committed plagiarism by using language or sentence structure that closely matches the original. See the Tips for Writers box below for ways to avoid plagiarism. (For advice on taking notes in the form of summaries, see p. 24. Another example of acceptable paraphrasing can be found on p. 95.)

Tips for Writers
Avoiding Plagiarism

If . . .		Then . . .
The information is common knowledge	→	You do not need a citation
The *words* are your own **and** The *idea* is your own	→	You do not need a citation
The *words* are someone else's	→	Place them in quotation marks **and** Include a citation
The *words* are your own **but** The *idea* is someone else's	→	Acknowledge the author of the idea by referring to him/her in the text **and** Include a citation

Note: This chart is adapted from *Academic Honesty, Plagiarism, and the Honor System: A Handbook for Students* (Washington, D.C.: Trinity Washington University, 2005), 2, and is used by permission.

6b-3 Downloading Internet sources carefully to avoid plagiarism

As with any other source, information derived from the Internet must be properly paraphrased and cited. A particular danger arises, however, from the ease with which Internet material can be downloaded into your working text. Whenever you download material from the Internet, be sure to create a separate document file for that material. Otherwise, Internet material may inadvertently become mixed up with your own writing. Moreover, you should keep in mind that Web sites are more volatile than print sources. Material on many Web sites is updated daily, and a site that you find early in your research may be revised or even completely gone by the time you write your final draft. Therefore, you should always record complete bibliographic information for each Internet source as you use it, as well as the date on which you accessed the site.

6c Plagiarism and the Internet

While plagiarism is not a new problem, the opportunities for plagiarism have increased exponentially with the growing popularity of and dependence on the Internet. Careless cut-and-paste practices, as noted above, pose a real hazard to unwary Internet users. A more distressing and significant problem, however, is the virtual explosion of Web sites offering students the opportunity to buy term papers or even download them for free. Often presenting themselves as sources of "research assistance," these sites afford countless possibilities for plagiarism under the guise of providing "help" to students who are "in a hurry," "under pressure," or "working on a deadline." Many of these Web sites bury in the "FAQs" (Frequently Asked Questions) or "About Us" sections the caveat that students should use the Web site's papers only as "models" for their own papers. They are, of course, quite right to include this warning. However, before you decide to use the "research assistance" these Web sites claim to provide, consider the criteria for evaluating Internet sources provided in Chapter 2 (see 2b-3).

Some professors forbid their students to use any Web sites in their research papers. If you are allowed and/or expected to incorporate Web-based material into your research, you need to take special care to make certain that the sites you are using are reliable. In determining the usefulness of a Web site, you should always ask about the author's credentials; for many of these "paper mill" sites, the author of the paper is anonymous and may even be another student. Why, then, should you trust the information the paper provides? Similarly, the Web site's URL should cause you to hesitate; paper mills typically have a .com extension, rather than the more trustworthy .edu or .gov extension that you might expect from a true academic site. You should also consider whether you would really want to list the site in your bibliography; it is not very likely that your professor will be impressed with a bibliographic entry for "schoolisrotten.com."

Finally, if you are ever tempted, you should also realize that if you found the Web site, the chances are good that your professor can find it too. It is not very hard—indeed, it is quite simple—for a professor to track down the source of a plagiarized paper. And remember: the consequences can be devastating.

Note: Ignorance about what constitutes plagiarism is not usually considered an acceptable excuse by college professors, school judicial associations, or university administrators. Read your school's policy on plagiarism and make sure you understand it. Finally, if you have any doubts or need clarification, ask your professors or consult a reference librarian.

7

Quoting and Documenting Sources

Any history paper you write reflects your careful reading and analysis of primary and secondary sources. This section offers general guidance on incorporating source material into your writing through quotation and paraphrase. It also explains the conventions historians use to cite and document sources.

7a   Using quotations

Quotations are an important part of writing in history. Quotations from primary sources provide evidence and support for your thesis. Quotations from secondary sources tell your readers that you are well informed about the current state of research on the issue that you are examining. The guidelines that follow will help you decide when to quote and how to use quotations effectively.

7a-1   When to quote

Some students go to extremes, producing papers that are little more than a series of quotations loosely strung together. No matter how interesting and accurate the quotations, such a paper is no substitute for your own analysis and discussion of sources. In general, you should minimize your use of quotations, and you should choose the quotations you do use with great care. When deciding if you should use a quotation, consider the following points.

Do not quote if you can paraphrase. Summarizing or paraphrasing in your own words is usually preferable to direct quotation; it demonstrates that you have digested the information from the source and made it your own. In particular, you should not quote directly if the quotation would provide only factual information. Examine this passage from *Slave Counterpoint*, a study of eighteenth-century African American culture:

ORIGINAL PASSAGE

Working alongside black women in the fields were boys and girls. Although the age at which a child entered the labor force varied from plantation to plantation, most masters in both Chesapeake and Lowcountry regarded the years of nine or ten as marking this threshold. . . . Black children, unlike their enslaved mothers, do not seem to have been singled out for any more onerous duties than their white counterparts. Those white children who left home to become servants in husbandry in early modern England generally did so at age thirteen to fourteen. However, they had probably been working for neighboring farmers on a nonresident basis from as young as seven.[1]

This passage contains a number of interesting facts. However, while it is clear and well written, there is nothing particularly significant about the wording of the passage per se; there are no striking analogies or turns of phrase that are particularly memorable. For this reason, a paraphrase is preferable to a direct quotation. The paraphrase that follows includes the important facts from the original but puts them in the writer's own words. As with all paraphrases, the model below includes a footnote to indicate the source of the information.

PARAPHRASE

Slave children began to work in the fields with their mothers at around the age of nine or ten. Their experiences as child laborers were similar to those of white children who worked in rural settings in England, where children as young as seven were sent to work on

1. Philip D. Morgan, *Slave Counterpoint: Black Culture in the Eighteenth-Century Chesapeake and Lowcountry* (Chapel Hill: University of North Carolina Press, 1988), 197.

nearby farms, and moved into the homes of their employers in their
early teens.[2]

    2. Philip D. Morgan, *Slave Counterpoint: Black Culture in the
Eighteenth-Century Chesapeake and Lowcountry* (Chapel Hill: University
of North Carolina Press, 1998), 197.

For additional information on paraphrasing without
plagiarizing, see 6b-2.

Do quote if the words of the original are especially memorable.
You might want to quote directly when your source says
something in a particularly striking way. Consider, for
example, the following passage from a student paper on
the cholera outbreak of 1854:

Steven Johnson argues that the densely packed population of London

provided ideal conditions for cholera bacteria to thrive. "London,"

he says, "offered *Vibrio cholerae* . . . precisely what it offered stock-

brokers and coffee-house proprietors and sewer-hunters: a whole new

way of making a living."[3]

    3. Steven Johnson, *The Ghost Map: The Story of London's Most
Terrifying Epidemic — and How It Changed Science, Cities, and the
Modern World* (New York: Riverhead Books, 2006), 96.

The quotation from Johnson is memorable because of
his use of anthropomorphism, which creates an image
that could not be duplicated in a summary or paraphrase.
The student, then, has chosen an effective quotation.

You might also wish to quote when the original words
are important to readers' understanding of the author's
intentions or feelings, as in the following example:

Fire was a serious danger in sixteenth-century cities. Entire neighbor-

hoods could be destroyed as a result of a single fire that grew out

of control. In fact, victims of violent crime knew that they should

call "Fire" rather than "Help" if they hoped someone would come to

the rescue. As A. Roger Ekirch puts it, "If murder or robbery failed to

animate their [neighbors'] sense of community, the threat of being

burned alive almost always did."[4]

    4. A. Roger Ekirch, *At Day's Close: Night in Times Past* (New York:
W. W. Norton and Company, 2005), 117.

In the quote that ends this passage, the tone is as important as the content. It would be impossible to capture in a summary or paraphrase the irony of the original.

7a-2 How to quote

When you quote, you must follow the conventions for using quotation marks and integrating quotations in the text of your paper. Keep in mind the following important points.

Frame your quotation. Quotations from sources cannot simply be dropped into your paper. Even if a quotation is properly cited (see 7b) and appropriate to a point you are making, you cannot assume your readers will immediately grasp where the quote comes from or why it is relevant. You must surround the quotation with text of your own that introduces the quote and explains its significance. This example is from a student paper on Judge Benjamin Lindsey, the founder of the first juvenile court in the United States:

INEFFECTIVE

Like most progressives, Lindsey was interested in social reform. "I found no 'problem of the children' that was not also the problem of their parents."[5]

---

5. Benjamin Barr Lindsey, *The Beast* (New York: Doubleday, 1910), 151.

In this example, the quotation is not clearly linked to the writer's statement that Lindsey was interested in social reform. Are readers meant to assume that Lindsey wanted to remove children from the homes of unfit parents? Provide government support for indigent parents? Encourage state-funded family counseling?

In the revised version, the student clearly introduces the quotation and frames it in a way that makes its significance clear:

EFFECTIVE

Addressing the source of juvenile crime, Lindsey wrote: "I found no 'problem of the children' that was not also the problem of their parents."[6] Thus, for Lindsey, the reform of the juvenile justice system was intrinsically linked to the reform of adult criminal courts.

---

6. Benjamin Barr Lindsey, *The Beast* (New York: Doubleday, 1910), 151.

In this revision, the significance of the quotation as it per-
tains to the writer's argument is clear. The writer's analysis before and after the quotation puts Lindsey's words in
context.

Indicate where your quotation begins and ends. When quoting a source, you should quote the source's words exactly,
and you should enclose the material from your source in
quotation marks. Commas and periods should always be
enclosed within the quotation marks; colons and semi-
colons should appear outside of the quotation; other end
punctuation (question marks and exclamation points)
should be enclosed within the quotation marks if they are
part of the quote and should appear outside if not.

Indent long quotations. If your quotation is four or more
typed lines, you should set it off by indenting it; this is
called a block quotation. Block quotations are single-
spaced and are not enclosed in quotation marks. Typically, long quotations are preceded by an introductory
sentence followed by a colon, as in this example:

> The comments of Chang Han, an official of the Ming dynasty, reflect
> the attitude of many of his contemporaries toward outsiders:
>
>> Foreigners are recalcitrant and their greed knows no bounds.
>> . . . What is more, the greedy heart is unpredictable. If one day
>> they break the treaties and invade our frontiers, who will be
>> able to defend us against them?[7]
>
> Despite this distrust, Jesuit missionaries were able to achieve posi-
> tions of honor and trust in the imperial court, ultimately serving the
> emperor as scholars and advisers.

---

7. Chang Han, "Essay on Merchants," trans. Lily Hwa, in *Chinese
Civilization and Society: A Sourcebook*, ed. Patricia Buckley Ebrey (New
York: Free Press, 1981), 157.

You should use block quotations sparingly. Frequent
use of long quotations suggests that you have not really
understood the material well enough to paraphrase.
Moreover, a long quotation can be distracting and cause
readers to lose the thread of your argument. Use a lengthy
quotation only if you have a compelling reason to do so.

Integrate your quotations grammatically. When you use a
direct quote, make sure that the resulting sentence is still
grammatically correct. You may need to change an initial
capital to lowercase, make a singular into a plural (or vice

versa), or add a word or phrase to make the meaning of the original clear in the context of your sentence. If you need to change or add a letter or word, use brackets to indicate the change. For example, in the quotation from A. Roger Ekirch on page 96, the antecedent of the pronoun *their* was no longer clear when the quote was taken out of its original context, so the writer has added the word *neighbors,* in brackets.

Note: While your *own* grammar and spelling should be accurate, you should *not* correct grammatical or spelling mistakes in the text you are quoting. Instead, indicate such mistakes by inserting the Latin word *sic* in brackets to indicate that the mistake occurs in the original and is not yours (see 5d).

Keep quotations brief. To keep quoted material to a minimum, you should condense quoted passages by using ellipsis points (three periods, with spaces between), which indicates that you have left out some of the original material. The passage quoting Steven Johnson on page 96 includes an example of this method. If you are leaving out material at the end of a sentence but what remains is grammatically a complete sentence, first type a period (with no space preceding it) and then the three evenly spaced ellipsis points. The passage quoting Chang Han on page 98 includes an example of this method.

7b Documenting sources

For all of the sources in your paper, including visual and other nonwritten materials, you must provide complete bibliographic information. This is important for two reasons. First, it gives appropriate credit to your sources. In addition, bibliographic information enables readers to look up your sources to evaluate your interpretation of them or to read more extensively from them.

7b-1 Footnotes and endnotes

Historians typically use footnotes or endnotes to document their sources. With this method, you place a raised number, called a *superscript*, at the end of the last word of a quotation, paraphrase, or summary. This number corresponds to a numbered note that provides bibliographic information about your source. Notes may be placed at the bottom of the page (footnotes) or at the end of the paper (endnotes). In either case, notes should be numbered consecutively from the beginning to the end of the paper. The following example shows a source cited in the text of a paper and documented in a footnote or endnote:

TEXT

Norton argues that "the witchcraft crisis of 1692 can be comprehended only in the context of nearly two decades of armed conflict between English settlers and the New England Indians."[8]

NOTE

  8. Mary Beth Norton, *In the Devil's Snare: The Salem Witchcraft Crisis of 1692* (New York: Alfred A. Knopf, 2002), 12.

You should ask your instructor if he or she has a preference for footnotes or endnotes. If the choice is left up to you, weigh the advantages and disadvantages of each form. Footnotes allow your readers to refer easily and quickly to the sources cited on a given page, but they can be distracting. Further, historians often use explanatory or discursive notes, which contain more than simple bibliographic information. (For an example of a discursive endnote, see endnote 4 from the model student paper on p. 131.) If your paper has a large number of discursive footnotes in addition to bibliographic footnotes, the pages might look overwhelmed with notes. If you use endnotes, you do not need to worry about the length of your notes. However, endnotes are less accessible, requiring readers to turn to the end of the paper to refer to each note.

7b-2 Bibliography

Papers with footnotes or endnotes also need to have a bibliography—a list of all the sources consulted or cited in the paper, arranged alphabetically by authors' last names (or by title where there is no author). In a paper with endnotes, the bibliography always follows the last endnote page. (See p. 132 for a sample bibliography.)

Note: An alternative form of documentation commonly used in professional journals in the social sciences is the author-date system. The author's last name and the publication date of a cited source are included in parentheses in the text itself; complete bibliographic information appears in a reference list at the end of the text. This form of documentation is not often used in history because the author-date system is generally not practical for documenting many of the primary sources historians use. Occasionally, a history professor may suggest the use of the author-date system for a book review or for a paper citing only one or two sources, but you should not use it unless you are specifically told to do so.

7b-3 Documenting nonwritten materials

Maps, graphs, photographs, cartoons, and other nonwritten materials can be useful in a history paper. It is not enough, however, to add these materials to your paper without discussion or explanation. When they appear in the body of a paper, visual materials, like quotations, should be incorporated into the text. Each image should include a caption that identifies it, and the text accompanying any visual material should explain its significance and its relationship to the topic of discussion. If you group visual materials in an appendix to your paper, you will also need to supply captions that identify the materials and their sources. Of course, using maps, photographs, and other nonwritten materials without full citations constitutes plagiarism. Like any other source, nonwritten materials must be cited in the bibliography.

7c Documentation models

The models in this section follow the notes and bibliography system set forth by *The Chicago Manual of Style*, 15th ed. (Chicago: University of Chicago Press, 2003), and Kate L. Turabian's *A Manual for Writers*, 7th ed. (Chicago: University of Chicago Press, 2007). The *Chicago* system is the format usually preferred by historians, and the one your history instructor will most likely ask you to follow. If you are uncertain, check your syllabus or ask your instructor for his or her preference.

7c-1 Formatting guidelines for footnotes and endnotes

As noted in 7b, historians provide notes, either at the bottom of each page (footnotes) or at the end of a text (endnotes) in order to acknowledge their sources and enable

Directory to Documentation Models

their readers to find the same sources for themselves. The following example illustrates the elements that should be included in a typical note when a source is referenced for the first time. Models for citing specific sources follow in 7c-3.

1. First reference to a source
All notes begin with a paragraph indent and are numbered consecutively throughout the paper. Individual notes should be single-spaced, with a double-space between notes. When a source is noted for the first time, you should include complete bibliographic information.

    1. Robert McGhee, *The Last Imaginary Place: A Human History of the Arctic World* (Oxford: Oxford University Press, 2005), 197.

2. Shortened forms in subsequent notes
As illustrated above, the first time you cite a source, you *must* provide complete bibliographic information. In subsequent notes, however, use a shortened form. There are two acceptable methods to shorten a reference. As one option, you can cite the author's last name followed by a comma and the page or pages cited.

    2. McGhee, 188.

Alternatively, you may include a shortened form of the title in your subsequent reference. This is necessary if you cite more than one work by the same author in your paper or if a subsequent note appears long after the first reference. To shorten the title, use the main word or words from the title of the work.

    2. McGhee, *Last Imaginary Place*, 76.

3. Using ibid. in subsequent notes
The abbreviation *ibid.* (from the Latin *ibidem*, meaning "in the same place") is sometimes used to refer to the work cited in the previous note. However, some professors and professional journals prefer the author/page or the author/short title/page style. Be sure you know which method your professor prefers.

When it is used, ibid. stands in place of both the author's name and the title of the work. If you are referring to the same page, use ibid. alone; if you are referring to different page numbers, use ibid. followed by a comma and the new page numbers. Do not use italics or underlining for ibid.

    3. Ibid., 79–84.

Note: Do not use ibid. if the previous note refers to more than one work.

7c-2 Formatting guidelines for bibliographies

Your bibliography is a list of the books, articles, and other sources you used in preparing your paper. It must include all the works you cited in your notes; it may also include other works that you consulted but did not cite. However, avoid the temptation to pad your bibliography; list only materials you did in fact use.

Note: If your bibliography is long, you may wish to divide it into sections, such as "Primary Sources" and "Books and Articles." If you have used manuscripts or other unpublished sources, you might list these separately as well.

4. Typical bibliography entry
The following example illustrates the elements that should be included in a typical bibliography entry. Models for citing a variety of specific sources can be found in 7c-3.

McGhee, Robert. *The Last Imaginary Place: A Human History of the Arctic World*. Oxford: Oxford University Press, 2005.

Bibliography entries are listed alphabetically by authors' last names; the first line of the entry begins at the far left, and subsequent lines are indented. Authors are listed last name first, followed by a comma and then the first names and initials (if any). Periods separate the author's name, title of the work, and publication information. Individual entries should be single-spaced, with a double-space between entries.

5. Multiple works by the same author
If your bibliography includes more than one work by the same author, use three hyphens followed by a period (---.) in place of the author's name in subsequent bibliographic entries. List books by the same author alphabetically by title.

McGhee, Robert. *Ancient People of the Arctic*. Vancouver: University of
British Columbia Press, 1996.

---. *The Last Imaginary Place: A Human History of the Arctic World*. Oxford:
Oxford University Press, 2005.

7c-3 Models for notes and bibliography entries

The following documentation models of notes and bibliography entries illustrate the types of sources commonly
used in history. The Directory to Documentation Models
on page 102 lists the various types of sources and the page
numbers where the models can be found. For each source,
the model note appears first, followed by a bibliography
entry for the same source. In the margins, an "**N**" signifies
that the model is formatted as a footnote; a "**B**" indicates a
bibliography format. For additional help with formatting
notes and bibliography entries, see 7c-1 and 7c-2.

Books

6. Basic form for a book
Include the author's name, the complete title (including
subtitle) in italics, the place of publication, the publisher's
name, and the publication date. (The Citation Guide on
page 107 illustrates how to find these elements in a book
and list them in the correct order.) Give page numbers for
footnotes and endnotes, but not for bibliography entries.

N   6. Psyche A. Williams-Forson, *Building Houses Out of Chicken Legs:
Black Women, Food, and Power* (Chapel Hill: University of North Carolina
Press, 2006), 135.

B   William-Forson, Psyche A. *Building Houses Out of Chicken Legs: Black
Women, Food, and Power*. Chapel Hill: University of North Carolina
Press, 2006.

7. Online book
Include all of the standard publication information available, as well as online publisher, date, and URL. If you
have accessed an online book through an authored Web
site, your note should also include the author, name, and
date of the Web site, if known. End your citation with the
date on which you accessed the site.

N   7. Alfred Russell Wallace, *Contributions to the Theory of Natural
Selection: A Series of Essays* (New York: Macmillan, 1871; Project
Gutenberg, 2007), 19, http://www.gutenberg.org/etext/22428 (accessed
November 4, 2008).

B   Wallace, Alfred Russell. *Contributions to the Theory of Natural Selection:
A Series of Essays*. New York: Macmillan, 1871; Project Gutenberg,
2007. http://www.gutenberg.org/etext/22428 (accessed November
4, 2008).

N   7. Cotton Mather, *Memorable Providences, Relating to Witchcrafts and
Possessions* (1689), at Douglas O. Linder, *Famous Trials*, http://www
.law.umkc.edu/faculty/projects/ftrials/salem/ASA_MATH.HTM (accessed
January 25, 2009).

B   Mather, Cotton. *Memorable Providences, Relating to Witchcrafts and
Possessions*. 1689. At Douglas O. Linder. *Famous Trials*. http://
www.law.umkc.edu/faculty/projects/ftrials/salem/ASA_MATH.HTM
(accessed January 25, 2009).

8. Two or more authors

List the authors in your note in the order in which their
names appear on the title page. In a bibliography entry,
list the first author's name in reverse order (last name
first), but give the names of other authors in the normal
order.

N   8. Toyin Falola and Matthew M. Heaton, *A History of Nigeria*
(Cambridge: Cambridge University Press, 2008), 262.

B   Falola, Toyin, and Matthew M. Heaton. *A History of Nigeria*. Cambridge:
Cambridge University Press, 2008.

Note: For a book with more than three authors, you may
use the Latin term *et al.* ("and others") after the first
author instead of listing all the authors in a footnote
or endnote (for example, Jane Doe et al.). Bibliographic
entries, however, must include all of the authors' names.

9. Author's name in the title

When an author's name appears in the title of a book, as
in an autobiography or a collection of letters or papers,
your footnote or endnote should begin with the title of
the book.

N   9. *Charles Darwin's Letters: A Selection, 1825–1859*, ed. Frederick
Burkhardt (Cambridge: Cambridge University Press, 1996), 15–19.

Begin the bibliography entry with the author's name,
even if it appears in the title.

B   Darwin, Charles. *Charles Darwin's Letters: A Selection, 1825–1859*. Edited
by Frederick Burkhardt. Cambridge: Cambridge University Press,
1996.

Citation Guide
Books

A typical citation for a book includes the information below, available from the title page and copyright page. In addition, page number(s) are included for notes but not for bibliography entries.

1 Author

2 Title and subtitle

3 City of publication

4 Publisher

5 Date of publication

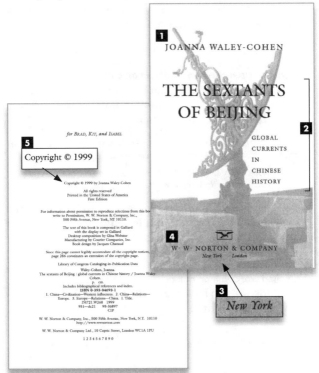

NOTE

1. Joanna Waley-Cohen, *The Sextants of Beijing: Global Currents in Chinese History* (New York: W. W. Norton & Company, 1999), 59–60.

BIBLIOGRAPHY

Waley-Cohen, Joanna. *The Sextants of Beijing: Global Currents in Chinese History*. New York: W. W. Norton & Company, 1999.

10. Anonymous work
For works with no known author, editor, or compiler, begin with the title.

N   10. *History of Organized Felony and Folly* (Whitefish, MT: Kessinger, 2003), 83.

In the bibliography, list the work by its title. If the title begins with an article (*a*, *an*, or *the*), alphabetize the book according to the first letter of the next word.

B   *History of Organized Felony and Folly*. Whitefish, MT: Kessinger, 2003.

11. Edited or compiled work without an author
Cite a book by its editor (abbreviated *ed.*) or compiler (abbreviated *comp.*) if no author appears on the title page (as in a collection or anthology).

N   11. M. Mohamed Salih, ed., *African Parliament: Between Governments and Governance* (New York: Palgrave Macmillan, 2005), 59–60.

B   Salih, M. Mohamed, ed. *African Parliament: Between Governments and Governance*. New York: Palgrave Macmillan, 2005.

Note: A book with multiple editors should be treated the same way as a book with multiple authors (see model 8 on p. 106); list the editors in the order in which they appear on the title page.

12. Edited work with an author
For a book with an author as well as an editor, the editor's name follows the title.

N   12. Efraim Karsh, *Empires of the Sand: The Struggle for Mastery in the Middle East, 1789–1923*, ed. Inari Karsh (Cambridge, MA: Harvard University Press, 1999), 303–4.

B   Karsh, Efraim. *Empires of the Sand: The Struggle for Mastery in the Middle East, 1789–1923*. Edited by Inari Karsh. Cambridge, MA: Harvard University Press, 1999.

13. Translated work
A translator's name, like an editor's, is placed after the title when an author's name is given. If a source has an editor and a translator, then list both.

N   13. Xie Bingying, *A Woman Soldier's Own Story*, trans. Barry Brissman and Lily Chia Brissman (New York: Columbia University Press, 2001), 296.

B   Bingying, Xie. *A Woman Soldier's Own Story*. Translated by Barry Brissman and Lily Chia Brissman. New York: Columbia University Press, 2001.

N   13. Roman Vishniac, *Children of a Vanished World*, S. Mark Taper Foundation Book in Jewish Studies, ed. Mara Vishniac Kohn, trans. Miriam Hartman Flacks (Berkeley and Los Angeles: University of California Press, 1999), 23.

B   Vishniac, Roman. *Children of a Vanished World*. S. Mark Taper Foundation Books in Jewish Studies. Edited by Mara Vishniac Kohn. Translated by Miriam Hartman Flacks. Berkeley and Los Angeles: University of California Press, 1999.

14. Multivolume work

If an individual volume of a multivolume work does not have its own title, the note should include the volume number cited and the page numbers after the publication information. If your paper references two or more volumes, the bibliography entry should list the number of volumes in the work (as in the first example below); if you reference only one of the volumes, the bibliography should list only the volume used (as in the second example below).

N   14. Bonnie S. Anderson and Judith P. Zinsser, *A Place of Their Own: Women in Europe from Prehistory to the Present*, rev. ed. (New York: Oxford University Press, 2000), 1:150–51.

B   Anderson, Bonnie S., and Judith P. Zinsser. *A Place of Their Own: Women in Europe from Prehistory to the Present*. Rev. ed. 2 vols. New York: Oxford University Press, 2000.

If a single volume in a multivolume work has a separate title, include the volume number and title directly after the general title.

N   14. Hermann Kinder and Werner Hilgemann, *The Penguin Atlas of World History*, vol. 1, *From Prehistory to the Eve of the French Revolution*, rev. ed. (New York: Penguin Books, 2004), 176.

B   Kinder, Hermann, and Werner Hilgemann. *The Penguin Atlas of World History*. Vol. 1, *From Prehistory to the Eve of the French Revolution*. Rev. ed. New York: Penguin Books, 2004.

15. Edition other than the first

If the text you are using is not the first edition, provide the edition number in your note and bibliography.

N   15. Leonard Thompson, *A History of South Africa*, 3rd ed. (New Haven, CT: Yale University Press, 2001), 263.

B   Thompson, Leonard. *A History of South Africa*. 3rd ed. New Haven, CT: Yale University Press, 2001.

16. Work in a series

Some books are part of a series: publications on the same general subject that are supervised by a general editor or group of editors. For such books, include the series title but not the name of the series editor(s).

N   16. Jeffrey Brown Ferguson, *The Harlem Renaissance: A Brief History with Documents*, Bedford Series in History and Culture (Boston: Bedford/ St. Martin's, 2008), 186–87.

B   Ferguson, Jeffrey Brown. *The Harlem Renaissance: A Brief History with Documents*. Bedford Series in History and Culture. Boston: Bedford/ St. Martin's, 2008.

Specific sections or documents within books

17. Foreword, preface, introduction, or afterword

If the author of the foreword, preface, introduction, or afterword is also the author of the book, include the title of the section you are citing (in lowercase) after the author's name and before the title. If you are citing an introduction or other material written by someone other than the author of the book, the writer you are citing is listed first.

N   17. Bernard Lewis, introduction to *From Babel to Dragomans: Interpreting the Middle East* (Oxford: Oxford University Press, 2004), 7.

B   Lewis, Bernard. Introduction to *From Babel to Dragomans: Interpreting the Middle East*. Oxford: Oxford University Press, 2004.

N   17. Richard Dawkins, foreword to *God, the Devil, and Darwin: A Critique of Intelligent Design Theory*, by Niall Shanks (Oxford: Oxford University Press, 2004), ix.

B   Dawkins, Richard. Foreword to *God, the Devil, and Darwin: A Critique of Intelligent Design Theory*, by Niall Shanks. Oxford: Oxford University Press, 2004.

18. Article or chapter in an edited work

Cite the author and title of the chapter or article first, followed by the title, editor, and publication information for the book in which it appears. Include the specific page number you are citing in the note and the complete range of page numbers for the article in the bibliography.

N   18. Bernard Hamilton, "The Impact of the Crusades on Western Geographical Knowledge," in *Eastward Bound: Travel and Travelers, 1050–1550*, ed. Rosamund Allen (Manchester: Manchester University Press, 2004), 18.

B   Hamilton, Bernard. "The Impact of the Crusades on Western Geographical Knowledge." In *Eastward Bound: Travel and Travelers, 1050–1550*, edited by Rosamund Allen, 15–34. Manchester: Manchester University Press, 2004.

19. Letter in a published collection

List the sender, recipient, and date of the communication, and then cite the collection as you would a book. Include the page number(s) in the note but not in the bibliography entry. The Citation Guide on page 112 illustrates how to find all of these elements from a primary text in a collection and put them in the correct order.

N   19. Private Arthur E. Stark to Carole Joyce Stark Blocker, January 2, 1944, *World War II Letters: A Glimpse into the Heart of the Second World War Through the Words of Those Who Were Fighting It*, ed. Bill Adler (New York: St. Martin's Press, 2002), 142.

If you cite only one letter from a collection, you may list it as an individual letter in your bibliography, beginning with the author's last name.

B   Stark, Arthur E. Private Arthur E. Stark to Carole Joyce Stark Blocker, January 2, 1944. In *World War II Letters: A Glimpse into the Heart of the Second World War Through the Words of Those Who Were Fighting It*, ed. Bill Adler. New York: St. Martin's Press, 2002.

If you cite several letters from the same collection, however, list only the collection in your bibliography.

B   Adler, Bill, ed. *World War II Letters: A Glimpse into the Heart of the Second World War Through the Words of Those Who Were Fighting It*. New York: St. Martin's Press, 2002.

20. Other primary sources in a published collection

Other than letters, *The Chicago Manual of Style*, 15th ed., does not provide specific guidance on how to cite primary sources contained in published collections, but the guidelines in model 18 will work in most situations. Note that titles of reprinted full-length works such as pamphlets should be in italics, not quotation marks. In some cases, it may also be helpful to provide the original date of the source (if known). The following example is for a seventeenth-century pamphlet reprinted in a book.

N   20. William Walwyn, *Toleration Justified and Persecution Condemned* (1646), in *The English Levellers*, ed. Andrew Sharp (Cambridge: Cambridge University Press, 1998), 26–27.

B   Walwyn, William. *Toleration Justified and Persecution Condemned*. 1646. In *The English Levellers*, edited by Andrew Sharp, 9–30. Cambridge: Cambridge University Press, 1998.

Citation Guide
Letters in published collections

A typical citation for a letter in a published collection includes the information below. In addition, page number(s) are included for notes but not for bibliography entries.

1 Author (or sender) of the letter

2 Recipient

3 Letter writer's location

4 Date

5 Title and subtitle of collection

6 Editor of collection

7 City of publication

8 Publisher

9 Date of publication

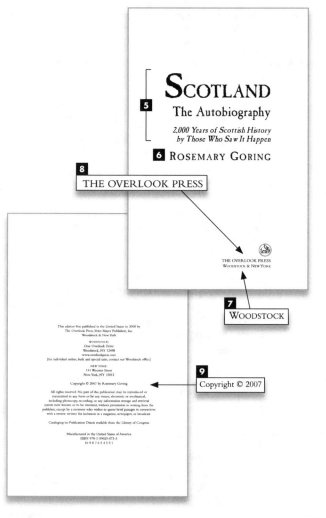

5

Scotland
The Autobiography

*2,000 Years of Scottish History
by Those Who Saw It Happen*

6 ROSEMARY GORING

8 THE OVERLOOK PRESS

THE OVERLOOK PRESS
WOODSTOCK & NEW YORK

7 WOODSTOCK

This edition first published in the United States in 2008 by
The Overlook Press, Peter Mayer Publishers, Inc.
Woodstock & New York

WOODSTOCK:
One Overlook Drive
Woodstock, NY 12498
www.overlookpress.com
[for individual orders, bulk and special sales, contact our Woodstock office]

NEW YORK:
141 Wooster Street
New York, NY 10012

Copyright © 2007 by Rosemary Goring

All rights reserved. No part of this publication may be reproduced or
transmitted in any form or by any means, electronic or mechanical,
including photocopy, recording, or any information storage and retrieval
system now known or to be invented, without permission in writing from the
publisher, except by a reviewer who wishes to quote brief passages in connection
with a review written for inclusion in a magazine, newspaper, or broadcast.

Cataloging-in-Publication Data available from the Library of Congress

Manufactured in the United States of America
ISBN 978-1-59020-073-5
10 9 8 7 6 5 4 3 2 1

9 Copyright © 2007

The Battle of Dunbar, 3 September 1650
1 OLIVER CROMWELL

*At the Battle of Dunbar Oliver Cromwell's Puritan army faced Scottish Coven-
anting troops outraged by the execution of Charles I. The encounter turned into
such a cruel and unnecessary rout that historian Thomas Carlyle dubbed it the
Dunbar Drove. Cromwell's army was ill, hungry and in a far inferior position,
but the Covenanting clergy urged their commander General David Leslie to
abandon his stand on the top of Doon Hill, and thus led their men into disaster.
As well as those killed, ten thousand or more were taken prisoner and suffered
appalling conditions as they were marched south or shipped abroad. Cromwell
wrote to Parliament the day after the battle to inform them of the outcome of the
battle.*

2

For the Honourable William Lenthal, Speaker of the Parliament of England,
These.

3 Dunbar, 4th September, 1650 **4**

Sir . . .

We having tried what we could to engage the Enemy, three or four miles West
of Edinburgh; that proving ineffectual, and our victual failing, – we marched
towards our ships for a recruit of our want. The Enemy did not at all trouble
us in our rear; but marched the direct way towards Edinburgh, and partly in
the night and morning slips-through his whole Army; and quarters himself in
a posture easy to interpose between us and our victual. But the Lord made him
to lose the opportunity. And the morning proving exceeding wet and dark, we
recovered, by that time it was light, a ground where they could not hinder us
from our victual: which was an high act of the Lord's Providence to us. We
being come into the said ground, the Enemy marched into the ground we were
last upon; having no mind either to strive to interpose between us and our
victuals, or to fight; being indeed upon this 'aim of reducing us to a' lock, –
hoping that the sickness of your Army would render their work more easy by
the gaining of time. Whereupon we marched to Musselburgh, to victual, and
to ship away our sick men; where we sent aboard near five-hundred sick and
wounded soldiers.

    And upon serious consideration, finding our weakness so to increase, and
the Enemy lying upon his advantage, – at a general council it was thought fit

NOTE

1. Oliver Cromwell to William Lenthal, Dunbar, September 4, 1650,
in *Scotland, the Autobiography: 2000 Years of Scottish History by Those
Who Saw It Happen*, ed. Rosemary Goring (Woodstock, NY: Overlook
Press, 2007), 85–88.

BIBLIOGRAPHY

Cromwell, Oliver. Oliver Cromwell to William Lenthal, Dunbar, September 4,
1650. In *Scotland, the Autobiography: 2000 Years of Scottish History
by Those Who Saw It Happen*, edited by Rosemary Goring. Woodstock,
NY: Overlook Press, 2007.

21. Illustration, table, or map

Give the item's title and author (if available) followed by the book title, author or editor, and publication information. In the note, give both the page number on which the item appears and any accompanying map, figure, table, or other number.

N   21. "The Contending Forces in Ireland, September 1643, with Selected Battlesites 1642–50," in *Divided Kingdom: Ireland 1630–1800*, by S. J. Connolly (Oxford: Oxford University Press, 2008), 502, map 2.

B   "The Contending Forces in Ireland, September 1643, with Selected Battlesites 1642–50." In *Divided Kingdom: Ireland 1630–1800*, by S. J. Connolly. Oxford: Oxford University Press, 2008.

If the item does not have its own title or author, list your note and bibliography entry according to the author or editor of the book in which it appears.

22. A source quoted in another source

If material you wish to use from a source has been taken from another source, it is always preferable to find and consult the original source. If this is not possible, you must acknowledge *both* the original source of the material *and* your own source for the information.

N   22. E. W. Creak, "On the Mariner's Compass in Modern Vessels of War," *Journal of the Royal United Services Institute*, vol. 33 (1889–90), 966, quoted in Alan Gurney, *Compass: A Story of Exploration and Innovation* (New York: Norton, 2004), 275–76.

B   Creak, E. W. "On the Mariner's Compass in Modern Vessels of War." *Journal of the Royal United Services Institute*, 33 (1889–90): 949–75. Quoted in Alan Gurney. *Compass: A Story of Exploration and Innovation*. New York: W. W. Norton, 2004.

Reference works

23. Dictionary or encyclopedia

In a note for a standard reference work that is arranged alphabetically, such as a dictionary or an encyclopedia, omit the publication information as well as the volume and page references. You must, however, note the edition if it is not the first. After the name and edition of the work, use the abbreviation *s.v.* (for *sub verbo*, "under the word") followed by the title of the entry in quotation marks.

N   23. *Encyclopaedia Britannica*, 15th ed. rev., s.v. "steam power."

N   23. *Merriam-Webster's Collegiate Dictionary*, 11th ed., s.v. "civilization."

Well-known reference works are usually not included in bibliographies.

24. Sacred texts
When referring to a passage from the Bible, cite the book (abbreviated), chapter, and verse(s), either in the text or in a note. Do not provide a page number. Identify the version in parentheses.

N   24. Matt. 20:4–9 (Revised Standard Version).

When referring to the Qur'an or other sacred work, use similar punctuation to refer to the parts of the text.

N   24. Qur'an 29:46.

Sacred texts are usually not included in bibliographies.

Periodicals

25. Basic form for a journal article (print)
Include the author's name, the title of the article in quotation marks, the name of the journal in italics, the volume number, the issue number (if available), and the date in parentheses. (For articles with two or more authors, see model 8 on p. 106.) In the note, include the page number(s) for the specific material you are citing; in the bibliography, include all the page numbers for the article. The Citation Guide on page 116 illustrates how to find all of these elements from a journal article and put them in the correct order.

N   25. Malcolm Gaskill, "Witchcraft and Evidence in Early Modern England," *Past and Present* 198 (February 2008): 62–63.

B   Gaskill, Malcolm. "Witchcraft and Evidence in Early Modern England." *Past and Present* 198 (February 2008): 33–70.

Some journals provide both volume and issue numbers. In the following model, the volume number is 283, the issue number is 5, the year of publication is 2000, and the page reference is 668.

N   25. Rhoda Wynn, "Saints and Sinners: Women and the Practice of Medicine throughout the Ages," *Journal of the American Medical Association* 283, no. 5 (2000): 668.

B   Wynn, Rhoda. "Saints and Sinners: Women and the Practice of Medicine throughout the Ages." *Journal of the American Medical Association* 283, no. 5 (2000): 668.

Citation Guide
Articles in print journals

A typical citation for an article accessed in a print journal
includes the information below.

1 Author
2 Title of article
3 Title of journal
4 Volume number

5 Issue number (if given)
6 Date of publication
7 Page numbers

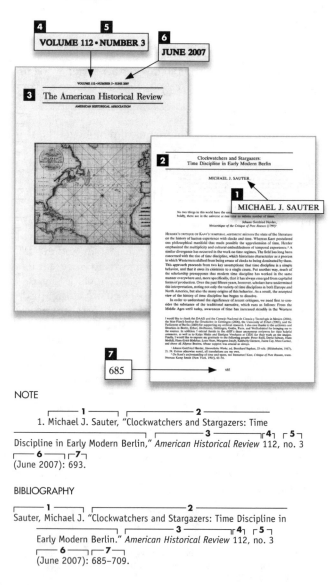

NOTE

1. Michael J. Sauter, "Clockwatchers and Stargazers: Time
Discipline in Early Modern Berlin," *American Historical Review* 112, no. 3
(June 2007): 693.

BIBLIOGRAPHY

Sauter, Michael J. "Clockwatchers and Stargazers: Time Discipline in
Early Modern Berlin." *American Historical Review* 112, no. 3
(June 2007): 685–709.

Note: You do not need to include the month or quarter of publication if you include the issue number, although it is not incorrect to do so.

26. Article in an online journal

Include the standard information for print articles: author's name, article title, journal title, journal number, publication date, and page number(s), if available. Also give the URL and the access date.

N   26. Tom Junes, "A Century of Traditions: The Polish Student Movement, 1815–1918," *Central and Eastern European Review* 2 (2008): 14, http://spaces.brad.ac.uk:8080/download/attachments/2868/Junes0507.pdf?version=1 (accessed September 3, 2008).

B   Junes, Tom. "A Century of Traditions: The Polish Student Movement, 1815–1918." *Central and Eastern European Review* 2 (2008): 1–26. http://spaces.brad.ac.uk:8080/download/attachments/2868/Junes0507.pdf?version=1 (accessed September 3, 2008).

27. Article accessed from a database

Include the standard information for a print article, along with the URL and the access date. (See the Citation Guide on page 118 for details.)

N   27. Robert Brent Toplin, "The Filmmaker as Historian," *American Historical Review* 93, no. 5 (1988): 1220, http://www.jstor.org/ (accessed June 13, 2008).

B   Toplin, Robert Brent. "The Filmmaker as Historian." *American Historical Review* 93, no. 5 (1988): 1210–27. http://www.jstor.org/ (accessed June 13, 2008).

If page numbers are not available, use another descriptive locator, such as a subheading or paragraph number in your note.

N   27. Cook, James W., "Seeing the Visual in U.S. History," *Journal of American History* 95, no. 2 (2008): paragraph 3, http://www.historycooperative.org/ (accessed November 23, 2008).

28. Article in a popular magazine

Include the author, title of the article, magazine title, and date (not in parentheses). Omit the volume and issue numbers. In the note, include the page number(s) of the specific material you are citing. You may, but are not required to, include the entire page range of the article in the bibliography; if you do, precede the page numbers with a comma, not a colon.

N   28. David Van Biema, "God vs. Science," *Time*, November 13, 2006, 50.

B   Van Biema, David. "God vs. Science." *Time*, November 13, 2006, 48–55.

Citation Guide
Articles in electronic databases

A typical citation for a journal article accessed from a database includes the information below, as well as the date of access.

1 Author
2 Title of article
3 Title of journal
4 Volume number
5 Issue number (if available)

6 Date of publication
7 Page number(s) (or other descriptive locators)
8 URL of database
9 Access date

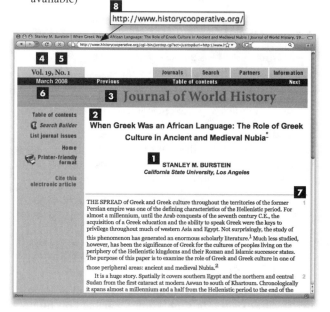

NOTE

┌─── **1** ───┐ ┌──────── **2** ────────
1. Stanley M. Burstein, "When Greek Was an African Language: The
┌──── **3** ────
Role of Greek Culture in Ancient and Medieval Nubia," *Journal of World*
┌**4**┐ ┌**5**┐ ┌── **6** ──┐ ┌── **7** ──┐ ┌──── **8** ────
History 19, no. 1 (March 2008): paragraph 3, http://www.history
┌──── **9** ────┐
cooperative.org/ (accessed May 27, 2008).

BIBLIOGRAPHY

┌─── **1** ───┐ ┌──────── **2** ────────
Burstein, Stanley M. "When Greek Was an African Language: The Role of
┌──── **3** ────
Greek Culture in Ancient and Medieval Nubia." *Journal of World*
┌**4**┐ ┌**5**┐ ┌── **6** ──┐ ┌──── **8** ────
History 19, no. 1 (March 2008). http://www.historycooperative.org/
┌──── **9** ────┐
(accessed May 27, 2008).

29. Newspaper article (print)

Cite the author's name (if it is given), the title of the article, the name of the newspaper, and the month, day, and year. If the city of the newspaper is not well known, include the state in parentheses. Each issue of a newspaper may go through several editions, and in each edition articles may be rearranged or even eliminated entirely. For this reason, you should cite the name of the edition in which the article appeared (for example, national edition, late edition). Page numbers are usually omitted, but ask your professor about his or her preference. If you are citing a large newspaper that is published in sections, include the name, letter, or number of the section.

N   29. Darryl Fears, "House Issues an Apology for Slavery," *Washington Post*, July 30, 2008, District and Maryland home edition, sec. A.

An individual newspaper article is usually not listed in a bibliography unless it is of particular importance to your argument or you refer to it often. If you do list a news article in your bibliography, use the following format:

B   Fears, Darryl. "House Issues an Apology for Slavery." *Washington Post*,
       July 30, 2008, District and Maryland home edition, sec. A.

30. Online news source

Include the author, if known; the title of the article; the name of the newspaper or online service; the date of publication; the URL; and the date of access, in parentheses.

N   30. Kate McGeown, "Burma: The Revolution That Didn't Happen," BBC News, September 26, 2008, http://news.bbc.co.uk/2/hi/asia -pacific/7635419.stm (accessed October 3, 2008).

B   McGeown, Kate. "Burma: The Revolution That Didn't Happen." BBC News,
       September 26, 2008. http://news.bbc.co.uk/2/hi/asia-pacific/
       7635419.stm (accessed October 3, 2008).

31. Book review (print)

Begin with the reviewer's name followed by the title of the review, if one is given. Follow this information by the words *review of*, the title of the work being reviewed, and its author. Also cite the periodical in which the review appears and the relevant publication information. If the author of the review is not named, begin with the title of the review or, if the review is untitled, with the words *Review of*.

N   31. Stanley Rosen, review of *Mao's Last Revolution*, by Roderick MacFarquhar and Michael Schoenhals, *American Historical Review* 112 (2007): 805.

B   Rosen, Stanley. Review of *Mao's Last Revolution*, by Roderick MacFarquhar and Michael Schoenhals. *American Historical Review* 112 (2007): 804–6.

32. Online review

Include the name of the reviewer (if available); the title and author of the book being reviewed; the name of the online publication; the date of the review; the URL; and the date of access, in parentheses.

N   32. Review of *Cherokee Thoughts, Honest and Uncensored*, by Robert J. Conley, *Publishers Weekly*, September 1, 2008, http://www.publishers weekly.com/article/CA6591186.html?industryid=47159 (accessed September 3, 2008).

B   *Publishers Weekly*. Review of *Cherokee Thoughts, Honest and Uncensored*, by Robert J. Conley. September 1, 2008. http://www.publishersweekly .com/article/CA6591186.html?industryid=47159 (accessed September 3, 2008).

Public documents

In the United States, most federal government publications are printed by the Government Printing Office in Washington, D.C., and may be issued by both houses of Congress (the House of Representatives and the Senate); by the executive departments (for example, the Department of State or the Department of the Interior); or by government commissions or agencies (for example, the Securities and Exchange Commission). A reference to a public document should include the name of the country, state, city, or county from which the document was issued (papers on U.S. history may omit *United States* or *U.S.*); the name of the legislative body, court, executive department, or other agency issuing the document; the title of the document or collection, if given; the name of the author, editor, or compiler; the report number; the publisher, if applicable (*Government Printing Office* may be shortened to *GPO*); the date; and the page or pages cited. The following models are for notes citing government documents commonly used by students writing history papers. For information on how to cite a government document accessed online, see model 38 on page 123.

33. Presidential papers

The public papers of the presidents of the United States have been published in two multivolume collections: *Compilation of the Messages and Papers of the Presidents, 1789–1897* for the early presidency and *Public Papers of the Presidents of the United States* for later presidents.

N   33. Dwight D. Eisenhower, *Public Papers of the Presidents of the United States: Dwight D. Eisenhower*, 1953 (Washington, DC: GPO, 1960), 228–30.

B   Eisenhower, Dwight D. *Public Papers of the Presidents of the United States: Dwight D. Eisenhower*, 1953. Washington, DC: GPO, 1960.

Note: Many presidential papers for the period 1789–present are also available online at *The American Presidency Project*, http://www.presidency.ucsb.edu/ws/. Complete public papers for George Herbert Walker Bush, William Jefferson Clinton, and George Walker Bush (January 1992–June 2004) are available online at http://www.gpoaccess.gov/pubpapers/index.html.

34. Executive department document

A note or bibliography entry for a document issued by one of the executive departments begins with the issuing department. Include the name of the author of the document, if it is known. For longer documents, it may be helpful to include page number(s), although this is not required. If the publication is part of a series, you may include the series number and omit the publication information.

N   34. U.S. Department of State, *Belarus*, Background Notes Series, no. 10344, 77.

B   U.S. Department of State. *Belarus*. Background Notes Series, no. 10344.

35. Testimony before a committee

Transcripts of testimony presented before congressional committees or commissions can be found in records called hearings. Begin the note with the committee or commission name.

N   35. House Committee on House Administration, *The Construction of the United States Capitol: Recognizing the Contributions of Slave Labor: Hearing before the Committee on House Administration*, 110th Cong., 1st sess., November 7, 2007, 55–56.

Bibliography entries should give U.S. Congress as the author, followed by the name of the branch of Congress, which can then be omitted from the beginning of the committee name.

B   U.S. Congress. House. Committee on House Administration. *The Construction of the United States Capitol: Recognizing the Contributions of Slave Labor: Hearing before the Committee on House Administration.* 110th Cong., 1st sess., November 7, 2007.

36. Congressional committee print
Both houses of Congress issue research reports called committee prints. Your note should include the committee print number and, if provided, the page number(s).

N   36. Senate Committee on Foreign Relations, *Managing Chaos: The Iraqi Refugees of Jordan and Syria and Internally Displaced Persons in Iraq,* 110th Cong., 2nd sess., 2008, Committee Print 44, 8.

B   U.S. Congress. Senate. Committee on Foreign Relations. *Managing Chaos: The Iraqi Refugees of Jordan and Syria and Internally Displaced Persons in Iraq.* 110th Cong., 2nd sess., 2008. Committee Print.

37. Treaty
U.S. treaties have been recorded in various publications since 1789. All references to treaties should include the treaty title (in quotation marks), the date on which the treaty was signed, and the name of the publication in which the treaty appears. Bibliographic entries should list the United States as the author.

Treaties from 1789 to 1873 can be found in *Statutes at Large of the United States of America, 1789–1873* (Stat.). A citation should include the volume number and any relevant part or section numbers. Treaties from 1874 to 1948 should list *United States Statutes at Large* as the publication. References to treaties in the latter collection should also note whether the treaty is found in the *Treaty Series* or *Executive Agreement Series* and should include the treaty number. Treaties from 1949 or later can be found in either *United States Treaties and Other International Agreements* (*UST*) or *Treaties and Other International Acts Series* (*TIAS*). References to these treaties should include the volume number and treaty number as well as the publication year, in parentheses; page numbers may be given.

N   37. "Treaty of Peace and Friendship with the Cherokees," July 2, 1791, *Statutes at Large of the United States of America* 8, art. 4.

B   United States. "Treaty of Peace and Friendship with the Cherokees." July 2, 1791. *Statutes at Large of the United States of America* 8, art. 4.

38. Online government publication

Include the author or issuing body and title of the document along with any available publication information such as document type, date, or document number. Also include the URL, and end with the date of access, in parentheses.

N   38. U.S. Department of State, *Country Reports on Terrorism 2007*, April 30, 2008, http://www.state.gov/s/ct/rls/crt/2007/index.htm (accessed August 7, 2008).

B   U.S. Department of State. *Country Reports on Terrorism 2007*. April 30, 2008. http://www.state.gov/s/ct/rls/crt/2007/index.htm (accessed August 7, 2008).

39. U.S. Constitution

In a footnote or endnote, the U.S. Constitution is cited by article (abbreviated *art.*) or amendment (*amend.*) and section (*sec.*). References to the Constitution should not be included in your bibliography.

N   39. U.S. Constitution, art. 4, sec. 1.

Multimedia sources

40. Film, videocassette, or DVD

Begin with the title of the film or series, followed by the type of medium (DVD or videocassette), the name of the director, and publication information. If you are citing a particular episode in a series or a scene in a DVD, you can include the title, using the same format as you would for a chapter in a book.

N   40. *Last Letters Home: Voices of American Troops from the Battlefields of Iraq (2004)*, DVD, directed by Bill Couturié (New York: HBO Home Video, 2005).

B   *Last Letters Home: Voices of American Troops from the Battlefields of Iraq (2004)*. DVD. Directed by Bill Couturié. New York: HBO Home Video, 2005.

41. Recorded interview

A citation for a published transcript of an interview should include the name of the person interviewed; the title of the interview (if any); the name of the person who conducted the interview; and the publication information for the source.

N   41. Joseph T. Glatthar, "General Lee's Army through Thick and Thin," interview by Peter S. Carmichael, *Civil War Times* 48, no. 1 (February 2009): 27.

B   Glatthar, Joseph T., "General Lee's Army through Thick and Thin." Interview by Peter S. Carmichael. *Civil War Times* 48, no. 1 (February 2009): 26-27.

If you heard the interview broadcast on radio or television, the note should include the name of the show and network on which the interview appeared. Broadcast interviews are not included in bibliographies.

N   41. President George W. Bush, interviewed by Bob Schieffer, *Face the Nation*, CBS, January 27, 2006.

For personal interviews, see model 47.

42. CD-ROM
Materials published on CD-ROM should be documented in the same way as printed works.

N   42. Naomi Reed Kline, *A Wheel of Memory: The Hereford Mappamundi*, CD-ROM (Ann Arbor: University of Michigan Press, 2001).

B   Kline, Naomi Reed. *A Wheel of Memory: The Hereford Mappamundi*. CD-ROM. Ann Arbor: University of Michigan Press, 2001.

43. Sound recording
Begin with the composer's name, followed by the title of the recording (italicized or underlined) and the name of the performer. Also provide the name of the recording company and the number. For an anonymous work or a collection of works by several composers, begin with the title of the recording.

N   43. Gustav Holst, *The Planets*, Royal Philharmonic Orchestra, André Previn, Telarc compact disc 80133.

B   Holst, Gustav. *The Planets*. Royal Philharmonic Orchestra. André Previn. Telarc compact disc 80133.

44. Online sound or video recording
Provide the necessary information about the recording as listed above. Also include any relevant descriptions about the original recording (such as duration and medium), the Web site that is hosting the material, the digital format, the URL, and the access date.

N   44. Heise, William. *Annie Oakley* (Edison Manufacturing Co., 1894), 21 sec.; 35 mm; from Library of Congress, *Inventing Entertainment: The Motion Pictures and Sound Recordings of the Edison Companies*,

MPEG, http://memory.loc.gov/ammem/edhtml/edhome.html (accessed September 1, 2008).

B Heise, William. *Annie Oakley*. Edison Manufacturing Co., 1894; 21 sec.; 35 mm. From Library of Congress, *Inventing Entertainment: The Motion Pictures and Sound Recordings of the Edison Companies*, MPEG, http://memory.loc.gov/ammem/edhtml/edhome.html (accessed September 1, 2008).

Unpublished sources

45. Unpublished thesis or dissertation

Include the author, title (in quotation marks), academic institution, and date.

N   45. J. W. Lee, "Paul and the Politics of Difference: A Contextual Study of Jewish-Gentile Difference in Galatians and Romans" (PhD diss., Union Theological Seminary, 2002), 67.

B Lee, J. W. "Paul and the Politics of Difference: A Contextual Study of Jewish-Gentile Difference in Galatians and Romans." PhD diss., Union Theological Seminary, 2002.

46. Unpublished letter in a manuscript collection

Begin with the name of the letter writer, followed by the name of the recipient and the date. Full identifying information about the collection in which the letter is found should follow, beginning with the file, box, or container number, if known; the name of the collection; and its location.

N   46. Nathaniel Hawthorne to James W. Beekman, April 9, 1853, letter box 3, James W. Beekman Papers, New-York Historical Society, New York.

If you have cited only one item from a collection, your bibliography entry should list it according to the item's author.

B Hawthorne, Nathaniel. Letter to James W. Beekman. James W. Beekman Papers. New-York Historical Society, New York.

If you have cited two or more items from a collection, the bibliography entry should cite the author and name of the collection, but not the specific items.

B Beekman, James W., Papers. New-York Historical Society, New York.

47. Personal interview

A note for an interview you have personally conducted should include the name of the person you interviewed;

the word *telephone*, if applicable; the words *interview by author*; the place of the interview, if applicable; and the interview date (you may abbreviate the month). Do not list personal interviews in your bibliography.

N   47. Jonathan Philips, telephone interview by author, August 4, 2008.

For published or broadcast interviews, see model 41.

48. Personal letter or e-mail
In your note, include the author's name, the type of communication, and the date of the communication. Do not list letters or e-mails in your bibliography.

N   48. Geoffrey Roberts, letter to author, October 6, 2007.

N   48. Michelle McSweeney, e-mail message to author, May 10, 2008.

Note: You should never include personal e-mail addresses in your citations.

Internet sources

For most documents accessed online—books, articles, multimedia, and so on—you should follow the formats given in the models above. To cite original material that exists only on the World Wide Web (other than online periodicals), you should include as much of the following material as possible: the author's name, the title of the document, the title or owner of the Web site, the URL, and the access date. The Citation Guide on page 127 illustrates how to find these elements from a Web site and put them in the correct order.

49. Material from a Web site with a known author
If the author of the material is known, list it at the beginning of the citation.

N   49. E. L. Skip Knox, "Results of the Fourth Crusade," *The Crusades*, http://crusades.boisestate.edu/4th/13.shtml (accessed September 2, 2008).

B   Knox, E. L. Skip. "Results of the Fourth Crusade." *The Crusades*. http://crusades.boisestate.edu/4th/13.shtml (accessed September 2, 2008).

50. Material from a Web site with an unknown author
If you are citing a Web site whose authorship is unknown, begin with the owner of the site.

Citation Guide
Information from Web sites

A typical citation for original material found on a Web site includes as much of the information below as possible, as well as the date of access.

1 Author or sponsoring institution

2 Title of the document or selection

3 Title of the site

4 URL

5 Access date

NOTE

1. Douglas Linder, "The Witchcraft Trials in Salem: A Commentary," *Famous Trials*, http://www.law.umkc.edu/faculty/projects/ftrials/salem/ SAL_ACCT.HTM (accessed October 31, 2008).

BIBLIOGRAPHY

Linder, Douglas. "The Witchcraft Trials in Salem: A Commentary." *Famous Trials*. http://www.law.umkc.edu/faculty/projects/ftrials/ salem/SAL_ACCT.HTM (accessed October 31, 2008).

50. Smithsonian Institution, "Dread History: The African Diaspora, Ethiopianism, and Rastafari," *Migrations in History*, http://www .smithsonianeducation.org/migrations/rasta/rasessay.html (accessed September 2, 2008).

B   Smithsonian Institution. "Dread History: The African Diaspora, Ethiopianism, and Rastafari." *Migrations in History*. http://www .smithsonianeducation.org/migrations/rasta/rasessay.html (accessed September 2, 2008).

51. Web forum or discussion list posting

In your note, include the author's name, the title of the thread (if any), the name of the list or forum, the date of the posting, the URL, and the date of access. In general, online forum and list postings are not included in bibliographies.

N   51. Paul Lovejoy, "Slavery in 'Traditional' Africa," posting to H-Africa Discussion Log, February 1, 2007, http://h-net.msu.edu/cgi-bin/ logbrowse .pl?trx=vx&list=h-africa&month=0702&week=a&msg=MPZbphNC UlJZe6joU0sWNg &user=&pw= (accessed June 14, 2008).

Note: You should never include personal e-mail addresses in your citations.

7d   Sample pages from a student research paper

Most of the suggestions in this book have been directed toward a single end: the production of a carefully researched, well-organized, and clearly written paper. On the following pages, you will find the title page, opening paragraphs, notes, and bibliography for one such paper.

SAMPLE TITLE PAGE

TO TRY A MONARCH:
THE TRIALS AND EXECUTIONS OF CHARLES I OF ENGLAND
AND LOUIS XVI OF FRANCE

 Lynn Chandler

History 362: Kings, Commoners, and Constitutions

November 22, 2008

1 Paper title, centered   3 Course title
2 Writer's name   4 Date

SAMPLE PAGE

Chandler 1

On January 30, 1649, Charles I, king of England, was beheaded.[1] The crowd around the scaffold greeted the sight of the severed head of their monarch with astonished silence. After lying in state for several days, the body was carried "in a Hearse covered with black Velvet, and drawn by six Horses, with four Coaches following it. . . ."[2] to Windsor Castle, where Charles was buried in royal estate beside Henry VIII and Queen Jane Seymour.[3] The scene was quite different on January 21, 1793, when another monarch ascended the scaffold--Louis XVI, king of the French. In place of the silence that followed Charles's execution, Louis's decapitation was announced with a "flourish of trumpets," and the executioner's cry of "Thus dies a Traitor!"[4] Contemporaries reported that the crowd surged forward, dipped their handkerchiefs in the king's blood, and ran through the streets shouting "Behold the Blood of a Tyrant!"[5] The body was wrapped in canvas and brought in a cart to the Tuileries, where Louis XVI, the former king of France, was buried like a commoner.[6] These two events, separated by almost a century and a half, appear at first glance to be totally isolated from each other. A careful review of both official documents and private accounts, however, reveals that the chief actors in the drama surrounding the execution of Louis XVI were not only aware of the English precedent, but referred to it again and again in the process of choosing their own courses of action, arguing for the validity of their point of view, and justifying their actions to the world.

The first clear-cut evidence that the French were influenced by the trial and execution of Charles I can be found in contemporary

---

1 Quotation shortened by using ellipsis, cited with endnote

2 Paraphrase cited with endnote

3 Writer's thesis

SAMPLE ENDNOTES PAGE

1   **2**

Notes

3   1. For a good general study of the execution, see Ann Hughes, "The Execution of Charles I," 2001, http://www .bbc.co.uk/history/british/civil_war_revolution/ charlesi_execution_01.shtml.

2. *England's Black Tribunal: The Tryal of King Charles the First* (printed for C. Revington, at the Bible and Crown in St. Paul's Churchyard, 1737), 55.

4   3. For a detailed account of the trial and execution of Charles I, see C. V. Wedgwood, *A Coffin for King Charles: The Trial and Execution of Charles I* (New York: Time Incorporated, 1966), and Graham Edwards, The Last Days of Charles I (Stroud, Gloucestershire: Sutton Publishing, 1999).

5   4. Joseph Trapp, *The Trial of Louis XVI* (London, 1793), 205.

6   5. Trapp, *Trial*, 206.

6. Trapp, *Trial,* 145. For a detailed account of the trial and execution of Louis XVI, see David P. Jordan, *The King's Trial: The French Revolution vs. Louis XVI* (Berkeley and Los Angeles: University of California Press, 1979).

7   7. Michael Walzer, ed., *Regicide and Revolution: Speeches at the Trial of Louis XVI*, trans. Marian Rothstein (Cambridge: Cambridge University Press, 1974), 1–89 passim.

8   8. Patricia Crawford, "'Charles Stuart, That Man of Blood,'" *Journal of British Studies* 16, no. 2 (1977): 53.

9. Wedgwood, *Coffin*, 89.

10. Susan Dunn, *The Deaths of Louis XVI: Regicide and the French Political Imagination* (Princeton, NJ: Princeton University Press, 1994), 59.

9   11. Jordan, *King's Trial*, 122.

12. John Hardman, *The French Revolution Sourcebook* (London: Arnold Publishers, 1999), 178.

---

1 First line of note indented ½ inch

2 Full-size note number followed by a period

3 Note for a Web site

4 Discursive (or content) note

5 Note for a book

6 Author and title shortened in subsequent reference

7 Author's name listed in normal order (first name, last name)

8 Note for a journal article

9 Notes are single-spaced; double-space between notes

SAMPLE BIBLIOGRAPHY

Bibliography

1 Crawford, Patricia. "'Charles Stuart, That Man of Blood.'" *Journal of British Studies* 16, no. 2 (1977): 41–61.

2 Dunn, Susan. *The Deaths of Louis XVI: Regicide and the French Political Imagination*. Princeton, NJ: Princeton University Press, 1994.

3 Edwards, Graham. *The Last Days of Charles I*. Stroud, Gloucestershire: Sutton Publishing, 1999.

England's Black Tribunal: The Tryal of King Charles the First. Printed for C. Revington, at the Bible and Crown in St. Paul's Churchyard, 1737.

4 Hardman, John. *The French Revolution Sourcebook*. London: Arnold Publishers, 1999.

5 Hughes, Ann. "The Execution of Charles I." http://www.bbc.co.uk/history/state/monarchs_leaders/charlesi_execution_01.shtml (accessed October 3, 2008).

6 Jordan, David P. "In Defense of the King." *Stanford French Review* 1, no. 3 (1977): 325–38.

---. *The King's Trial: The French Revolution vs. Louis XVI*. Berkeley and Los Angeles: University of California Press, 1979.

Trapp, Joseph. *The Trial of Louis XVI*. London, 1793.

Walzer, Michael, ed. *Regicide and Revolution: Speeches at the Trial of Louis XVI*. Translated by Marian Rothstein. Cambridge: Cambridge University Press, 1974.

1 First line of each entry at left margin; indent subsequent lines ½ inch
2 Single-space entries; double-space between entries
3 List entries alphabetically by authors' last names
4 Bibliography entry for a book
5 Bibliography entry for a Web site
6 Bibliography entry for a journal article

Appendix A

WRITING GUIDES OF INTEREST TO HISTORIANS

The following books offer guidance on stylistic matters and other writing concerns. The guides to writing in history, in addition to offering general advice, discuss how historians work and cover typical assignments, stylistic conventions, the research process, and documentation.

General writing guides

Hacker, Diana. *A Pocket Style Manual*. 5th ed. Boston: Bedford/St. Martin's, 2008. Also available at http://www.dianahacker.com/pocket.

Strunk, William, Jr., and E. B. White. *The Elements of Style Illustrated*. New York: Penguin Press, 2007.

Turabian, Kate L., Alice Bennett, and John Grossman. *A Manual for Writers of Research Papers, Theses, and Dissertations*. 7th ed. Chicago: University of Chicago Press, 2007.

University of Chicago Press. *The Chicago Manual of Style*. 15th ed. Chicago: University of Chicago Press, 2003.

Guides to writing in history

Benjamin, Jules R. *A Student's Guide to History*. 11th ed. Boston: Bedford/St. Martin's, 2010. Also available at http://www.bedfordstmartins.com/benjamin.

Marius, Richard, and Melvin E. Page. *A Short Guide to Writing about History*. 6th ed. New York: Pearson Education, 2007.

Mills, Elizabeth Shown. *Evidence Explained: Citing History Sources from Artifacts to Cyberspace*. Baltimore, MD: Genealogical Publishing, 2007.

Storey, William Kelleher. *Writing History: A Guide for Students*. 3rd ed. New York: Oxford University Press, 2008.

Internet guides for historians

Gevinson, Alan, Kelly Schrum, and Roy Rosenzweig. *U.S. History Matters: A Student Guide to U.S. History Online*. 2nd ed. Boston: Bedford/St. Martin's, 2009.

Trinkle, Dennis A., and Scott A. Merriman. *American History Highway: A Guide to Internet Resources on U.S., Canadian, and Latin American History*. Armonk, NY: M. E. Sharpe, 2007.

———. *The History Highway: A 21st Century Guide to Internet Resources*. Armonk, NY: M. E. Sharpe, 2006.

Appendix B

GUIDE TO SELECTED PRINT AND ONLINE RESOURCES IN HISTORY

By Susan Craig Murray, Valencia Community College

This appendix lists selected encyclopedias, dictionaries, indexes, and guides as well as a sampling of electronic research resources available through the Internet. Although accessing material online has the advantage of speed and convenience, do not underestimate the importance of working with established print sources such as encyclopedias and scholarly books during the research process.

Print resources

The materials listed here are not available at all libraries, but they give you an idea of the range of resources available. Remember, too, that librarians are an extremely helpful resource. They know their own collections well and can direct you to useful materials throughout your research process.

Overviews and encyclopedias

THE AMERICAS

Canadian Encyclopedia. Toronto: McClelland & Stewart, 2000.

In more than ten thousand articles, this unabridged volume covers all topics relevant to Canada. A free, regularly updated version is available online at http://www.thecanadian encyclopedia.com.

Encyclopedia of African-American Culture and History: The Black Experience in the Americas. 2nd ed. Detroit: MacMillan Reference Books, 2006.

This six-volume set offers almost 1,300 entries on black history and life in the United States, the Caribbean, and Latin America. Includes references, thematic list of entries, primary documents, photographs, statistics, and an index.

Encyclopedia of African American History, 1619–1895, and *Encyclopedia of African American History, 1896 to the Present*. New York: Oxford University Press, 2006, 2009.

These three- and five-volume sets offer a total of almost two thousand biographical and topical articles on African American history. Includes references, illustrations, charts, tables, maps, primary source documents, chronologies, cross-references, and an index.

Encyclopedia of American History. New York: Facts on File, 2003.

The eleven volumes in this set are chronologically arranged and contain more than three thousand entries on American history from the earliest human settlements to the twenty-first century. Includes bibliographies, cross-references, photographs, illustrations, maps, cartoons, and an index.

Encyclopedia Latina: History, Culture, and Society in the United States. Danbury, CT: Grolier Academic Reference, 2005.

The more than 650 topical and biographical articles in this four-volume set cover Latino history in the United States since the sixteenth century. Includes photographs, maps, appendices, Web resources, references, and an index.

Encyclopedia of the Middle Passage: Greenwood Milestones in African American History. Westport, CN: Greenwood Press, 2007.

This volume includes more than two hundred articles covering "the experience of slaves on the transatlantic ships" en route from Africa to the Americas during the fifteenth to the nineteenth centuries. Includes references, illustrations, maps, a chronology, and an index.

Mexico: An Encyclopedia of Contemporary Culture and History. Santa Barbara, CA: ABC-CLIO, 2004.

This overview of twentieth- and twenty-first-century Mexico explores political, economic, social, and cultural history. Includes maps, illustrations, bibliographies, and an index.

Native American Encyclopedia: History, Culture, and Peoples. New York: Oxford University Press, 2000.

This volume examines the history and culture of more than two hundred Native North American groups. Includes illustrations, maps, bibliographies, a pronunciation guide, a glossary, and an index.

Oxford Companion to Canadian History. Don Mills, ON: Oxford University Press, 2004.

This guide covers "the main events, institutions, places, and people" in Canadian history. Includes cross-references, lists of leaders, maps, and an index.

WORLDWIDE

Cambridge History of Russia. Cambridge: Cambridge University Press, 2006.

This three-volume set covers Russian history from c. 900 to the twentieth century; it is generally organized chronologically but also has thematic entries. Includes maps, illustrations, bibliographies, and an index.

China: Its History and Culture. 4th ed. New York: McGraw-Hill, 2005.

This volume covers the origins and early history of China through the early twenty-first century. Includes maps, illustrations, bibliographies, and an index.

Companion to Japanese History. Malden, MA: Blackwell, 2007.

This survey of Japanese history provides "an authoritative overview of current debates and approaches." Includes a chronology, thematic articles, references, and an index.

Encyclopedia of the Arab-Israeli Conflict: A Political, Social, and Military History. Santa Barbara, CA: ABC-CLIO, 2008.

This four-volume set looks at the Arab-Israeli conflict from a variety of perspectives, including political, cultural, religious, and military. Includes illustrations, maps, bibliographies, primary documents, and an index.

Encyclopedia of Historic Places. Rev. ed. New York: Facts on File, 2007.

This three-volume set has more than nine thousand entries on historically significant "cities, towns, districts, territories, and nations around the world." New and revised entries emphasize the impact of modern technology and industrial development on geography. Includes photographs, references, and an index by region.

Encyclopedia of the Modern Middle East and North Africa. 2nd ed. Detroit: Macmillan Reference USA, 2004.

This four-volume set details the anthropological, economic, religious, political, and social history of each country in the Middle East and North Africa. Offers maps, illustrations, topical outlines, genealogies, bibliographies, cross-references, a glossary, and an index. Also available as an e-book by subscription at select libraries.

Encyclopedia of World History. New York: Facts on File, 2008.

This seven-volume set covers prehistory to the present. Includes references, illustrations, maps, thematic essays, primary source documents, recommended readings for further study, a chronology, and an index.

History of the Ancient Near East, c. 3,000–323 BC. 2nd ed. Malden, MA: Blackwell, 2006.

This 368-page volume briefly examines the ancient history of Near East civilizations. Includes references, illustrations, charts, maps, a selection of Near Eastern texts in translation, and an index.

India: The Definitive History. Boulder, CO: Westview Press, 2007.

This volume examines the history of India from ancient to modern times. Includes maps, references, a chronology, and an index.

The Middle East. 11th ed. Washington, DC: CQ Press, 2007.

This overview of the Middle East covers the Arab-Israeli conflict, U.S. policy, the Persian Gulf, oil, Islam, and country profiles. This edition includes new chapters on Turkey and the Palestinian Authority as well as additional information on Afghanistan and Pakistan. Includes maps, tables, documents, an index, and a chronology.

New Encyclopedia of Africa. Detroit: Thomson/Gale, 2008.

This five-volume set explores African history from the earliest civilizations to the present day. Includes a thematic outline, photographs, references, maps, an appendix of ethnic and identity groups, and an index.

Oxford History of Britain. Rev. ed. Oxford: Oxford University Press, 2001.

This chronologically arranged volume covers British history for the past two thousand years. Includes maps, illustrations, genealogies, bibliographies, and an index.

Renaissance and Reformation. New York: Marshall Cavendish, 2007.

This six-volume set comprises 158 articles on the European Renaissance and Reformation, covering the period from 1300 to 1700. Although the focus is on Europe, it also includes major worldwide events of the period. Includes maps, illustrations, a timeline, a glossary, references, and an index.

Routledge Companion to European History Since 1763. London: Routledge, 2005.

This volume covers history up to the twenty-first century. Includes chronologies, biographies, maps, bibliographies, a glossary, and an index.

Topical dictionaries

THE AMERICAS

African American National Biography. New York: Oxford University Press, 2008.

This eight-volume set presents more than four thousand articles on the lives of African Americans from 1529 to the present. Includes photographs, suggested readings, bibliographies, and an index.

Canadian Oxford Dictionary. 2nd ed. Toronto: Oxford University Press, 2004.

In addition to definitions, which are based on Canadian English usage, this volume includes short biographical and geographical entries, a style guide, and a list of governors and prime ministers.

The Great American History Fact-Finder: The Who, What, Where, When, and Why of American History. 2nd ed. Boston: Houghton Mifflin, 2004.

This volume presents more than two thousand entries pertinent to the history and culture of the United States. Topics include political, legal, and military history; sports; arts and entertainment; and business. Includes maps, tables, suggested readings, primary documents, and an index.

Historical Dictionary of Ancient South America. Lanham, MD: Scarecrow Press, 2008.

With more than seven hundred entries, this volume explores the lives of people in South America during pre-Columbian times; it also covers well-known archaeologists who have studied ancient South American civilizations. Includes a chronology, an introduction, and a bibliography.

Historical Dictionary of Mexico. 2nd ed. Lanham, MD: Scarecrow Press, 2008.

This reference work covers the history of Mexico from pre-Columbian times through 2006. Includes a chronology, maps, and a bibliography, as well as hundreds of entries on topics relevant to Mexican history.

Historical Dictionary of United States–Middle East Relations. Lanham, MD: Scarecrow Press, 2007.

This text includes cross-referenced entries on important events, people, and issues in U.S.-Middle Eastern diplomatic relations from the Cold War to the present. Includes maps, illustrations, a chronology, and a bibliography.

WORLDWIDE

Columbia World Dictionary of Islamism. New York: Columbia University Press, 2007.

In over two thousand entries, this dictionary examines the history of Islam and Islamic countries. In addition to documenting people, places, and religious terms, this source addresses questions about Islamic fundamentalism and its place in modern society.

Dictionary of Battles and Sieges: A Guide to 8,500 Battles from Antiquity through the Twenty-First Century. Westport, CN: Greenwood Press, 2007.

This three-volume set contains entries for more than 8,500 battles from 1468 BCE to 2003. Each entry includes the battle's dates, context, military leaders, and outcome. Includes cross-references, a chronology, and an index.

Dictionary of the Middle Ages. New York: Scribner, 1982–89; 2003 supplement.

This is the single most complete source covering people, events, ideas, movements, texts, and cultural features of the medieval world. The thirteen-volume set covers 500 CE to 1500 CE. The supplement volume adds more than three hundred topics to broaden and update the coverage, adding more detail on women and gender issues, numerous first-time biographies, and new scholarship on social issues.

Holocaust Survivors: A Biographical Dictionary. Westport, CN: Greenwood Press, 2007.

This two-volume set offers 278 entries on the lives of more than five hundred individual and family survivors. Includes photographs, bibliographies, maps, a chronology, a glossary, and an index.

Oxford Dictionary of National Biography: In Association with the British Academy. From the Earliest Times to the Year 2000. Oxford: Oxford University Press, 2004.

This sixty-one-volume set provides more than fifty thousand biographies of men and women throughout the world "who shaped all aspects of the British past over the last 2,400 years." Also available online by subscription at select libraries.

Routledge Dictionary of Modern British History. London: Routledge, 2006.

This guide to the last 250 years includes all prime ministers, democratization, protest movements, and military conflict.

Atlases, chronologies, and timetables

THE AMERICAS

African American Chronology: Chronologies of the American Mosaic. Westport, CT: Greenwood Press, 2006.

This chronology of African American history covers the fifteenth to the twenty-first centuries. Includes references, a glossary, and an index.

Americas: The Changing Face of Latin America and the Caribbean. 3rd ed. Berkeley: University of California Press, 2006.

A companion volume to the PBS series, this chronology studies the history of Latin America and the Caribbean from a variety of perspectives, including social, political, cultural, religious, and economic. Includes maps, illustrations, references, and an index.

Atlas of American History. Rev. ed. New York: Facts on File, 2007.

This atlas covers American history from prehistory to the war on terrorism, exploring military, social, and religious history as well as patterns of migration. Aligned with the National Standards for United States History. Includes maps, illustrations, photographs, charts, graphs, and an index.

Atlas of Asian American History. New York: Checkmark Books, 2002.

This atlas explores the political, cultural, and social history of Asian Americans. Includes photographs, maps, charts, a bibliography, and an index.

Chronology of American Indian History. Updated edition. New York: Facts on File, 2007.

With over 1,400 entries, this chronology covers the history of Native North American life and culture from 25,000 BCE to 2006 CE. Includes references, maps, illustrations, a glossary, and an index.

WORLDWIDE

An Atlas of World Affairs. 11th ed. London: Routledge, 2007.

This atlas "describes the people, factions, and events that have shaped the modern world from World War II to the present day." This most recent edition covers new issues such as the war on terrorism, the expansion of the European Union, and the increased importance of environmental concerns. Includes maps, illustrations, references, and an index.

Cassell's Chronology of World History: Dates, Events, and Ideas That Made History. London: Weidenfeld & Nicolson, 2005.

This overview of world history offers essays on events, peoples, and themes.

A Concise History of the World Since 1945: States and Peoples. Basingstoke, UK: Palgrave Macmillan, 2006.

This volume focuses on "key topics such as human migration, science and technology, international business, religion and politics, and the breakup of Europe's overseas empires." Includes references, suggested readings, and an index.

Historical Atlas of Empires: From 4000 BC to the 21st Century. London: Mercury Books, 2004.

Spanning six thousand years, this atlas "shows that our modern global society is the direct result of accumulated effects of the empires of yesteryear." Includes maps, timelines, illustrations, and an index.

Leadership: Fifty Great Leaders and the Worlds They Made. Westport, CN: Greenwood Press, 2008.

This book profiles important figures in a variety of fields from ancient history through modern times. Includes illustrations, references, and an index.

The Penguin Historical Atlas of the Medieval World. London: Penguin Books, 2005.

This 144-page atlas covers the history of European peoples, cultures, and faiths from the fourth to the sixteenth centuries. The book uses timelines, maps, reproductions, and photographs to illustrate significant historic events "from the fall of the Roman Empire to the foundations of modern European civilization."

Routledge Atlas of British History: From 45 BC to the Present Day. 4th ed. London: Routledge, 2007.

The maps and illustrations in this atlas cover the political, military, economic, industrial, religious, social, and ethnic history of Great Britain and Ireland.

Internet resources

The Internet is an important research tool and is an increasingly useful place to find primary sources and full-text documents. You can view photographs and drawings, play audio recordings of speeches or U.S. Supreme Court arguments, or find historical articles and documents. As you use the Internet for research, be sure to assess the value of the material you find (see 2b-3) and to document where you found it (see 7c). The Web sites listed represent only a sampling of the extensive history sources available. For guides to using the Internet for historical research, see Appendix A.

Google. http://www.google.com

One of the most widely used search engines, Google returns fairly useful search results with simple searches, and more specific results with advanced search features. In addition, Google offers two useful areas for academic researchers: Google Book Search and Google Scholar.

Google Book Search. http://www.google.com/books

 This specialized area of Google allows full-text searching of books from thousands of publishers worldwide and provides links allowing users to buy the book or find it in a nearby library. For some older titles that are in the public domain, links to free downloads are provided.

Google Scholar. http://scholar.google.com

 This Google tool filters out non-academic content and allows you to set limiters on your search (e.g., keyword, publication title, author, date, and subject), mimicking the experience of an academic database search. As with Google Book Search, search results here link to preview pages that allow users to purchase or borrow the item; full text is available for many public domain items.

Note: No discussion of Internet resources would be complete without the mention of *Wikipedia*. Links to its more than two million articles come up frequently in online searches. Although much found within it may be reliable, *Wikipedia* describes itself as "the free encyclopedia that anyone can edit." In addition, *Wikipedia* emphasizes that it cannot "guarantee the validity of the information" it contains, and notes that no one associated with *Wikipedia* is "responsible for the appearance of any inaccurate . . . information." Thus said, it should not be cited in any academic research paper (see 2b-3).

General research gateways

Many university history departments have established research gateways to lead students to quality online resources. In addition, many independent sites act as übergateways, providing a collection of links to the best online academic and institutional Web sites available. The following are some of the more thorough gateways that allow public access.

AcademicInfo. http://www.academicinfo.net/hist.html
Best of History Web Sites. http://www.besthistorysites.net
Cornell University Library, Olin & Uris Libraries: Research Guide for History. http://www.library.cornell.edu/olinuris/ref/history .html
eHistory (Ohio State University). http://ehistory.osu.edu/osu/
The History Guide: Resources for Historians. http://www .historyguide.org/resources.html
History Matters: WWW History. http://historymatters.gmu.edu/ browse/wwwhistory/
Rutgers University Libraries: History—North America. http://www .libraries.rutgers.edu/rul/rr_gateway/research_guides/ history_us/history_us.shtml
A Student's Online Guide to History Reference Sources. http://bcs .bedfordstmartins.com/benjamin
University of Florida, George A. Smathers Libraries: History. http:// www.uflib.ufl.edu/hss/ref/history.html

Specialized sites for historical research

NORTH AMERICA

AcademicInfo: Canadian History Gateway. http://www
.academicinfo.net/canhist.html

> This site provides an annotated directory of online resources
> for the study of Canadian history. The Reference Desk offers
> links to Canadian archival resources, government docu-
> ments, and secondary sources such as the *Canadian Encyclope-
> dia Online* and the *Historical Atlas of Canada.*

AMDOCS: Documents for the Study of American History. http://
www.vlib.us/amdocs/

> This site contains primary source documents for the study of
> American history from c. 835 to 2009.

American Periodicals Series Online. First release 1741–1800. Ann
Arbor: ProQuest Information and Learning Company, 2000–.

> This site, which is based on the American Periodicals Series
> microform collection, provides digitized images of the origi-
> nal pages of articles from more than one thousand American
> scholarly, scientific, and popular magazines and journals
> published between 1740 and 1900. It is available by library
> subscription only.

The Avalon Project: Documents in Law, History and Diplomacy.
http://avalon.law.yale.edu/

> This site, sponsored by Yale Law School's Lillian Goldman
> Law Library, provides access to primary source materials in
> the fields of law, history, economics, politics, diplomacy, and
> government from 122 BCE to 2003 CE. Links to documents
> mentioned in the sources are also provided.

*Born in Slavery: Slave Narratives from the Federal Writers' Project,
1936–1938.* http://lcweb2.loc.gov/ammem/snhtml

> This part of the Library of Congress's American Memory Proj-
> ect contains over 2,300 first-person narratives originally col-
> lected in the 1930s. This collection also includes more than
> five hundred photographs of former slaves.

CET: Asian American History Resources. http://www.cetel.org/res
.html

> This site from the Center for Educational Telecommuni-
> cations provides links to print, online, and visual media
> resources for the study of Asian American history and culture.

Congressional Record. Washington, DC: GPO, 1873–. http://www
.gpoaccess.gov/crecord/index.html

> The *Congressional Record* covers debates and proceedings of
> Congress. Earlier series were called *Debates and Proceedings,*
> generally known as *Annals of Congress* (1789–1824), *Register of
> Debates* (1824–1837), and *Congressional Globe* (1833–1873).

Dictionary of Canadian Biography Online. http://www.biographi
.ca/index-e.html

> This site provides an introduction to the people and culture
> of Canada. Biographical information is provided for persons

who died or were last referenced between the years 1000 and 1930. Search by name, geographical location, or topical subdivision.

Digital History. http://www.digitalhistory.uh.edu

Developed through partnerships with the University of Houston, this site provides resources for the study of U.S. history from the Revolutionary War to the present. Includes primary sources, ethnic voices, interactive timelines, and reference material.

Documenting the American South. http://docsouth.unc.edu

This site contains digitized primary sources pertaining to the history, culture, and literature of the South. Includes texts, images, and audio files.

Documents from the Women's Liberation Movement. http://scriptorium.lib.duke.edu/wlm

Duke University's Special Collections Library sponsors this collection of online documents from the late 1960s to the early 1970s.

Internet Modern History Sourcebook. http://www.fordham.edu/halsall/mod/modsbook.html

This site, part of the Internet History Sourcebooks Project, provides access to thousands of primary sources for North American and world history from the Reformation to the twenty-first century. Includes links to external sites on related topics such as colonial North America, U.S. immigration, Canada, and U.S. society.

Jewish Women's Archive. http://jwa.org/

This site provides documents, films, oral histories, and other materials for the study of the history of American Jewish women.

Library of Congress. http://www.loc.gov/index.html

The Web site for the Library of Congress includes the American Memory Project, Global Gateway to World Culture and Resources, and current historical legislative information.

The Library of Congress: American Memory. http://memory.loc.gov/ammem/amhome.html

This site contains more than 130 multimedia collections of digitized documents, photographs, recorded sound, and moving pictures on important American historical events.

Presidential Libraries. http://www.archives.gov/presidential-libraries

This National Archives site provides access to presidential documents and links for presidential libraries from Herbert Hoover to George W. Bush.

Public Papers of the Presidents of the United States. http://www.gpoaccess.gov/pubpapers/search.html

This Government Printing Office site contains U.S. presidents' public papers and speeches; the material within each *Public Papers* volume is organized chronologically.

Repositories of Primary Sources. http://www.uiweb.uidaho.edu/
special-collections/Other.Repositories.html

This site lists more than five thousand links to Web sites that
house primary source materials for the study of North American and world history.

WORLDWIDE

Africa: History. http://www.africa.upenn.edu/About_African/
ww_hist.html

Sponsored by the University of Pennsylvania, this site links
to primary and secondary sources in African history.

AlexanderPalace.org: Russian History Website. http://www
.alexanderpalace.org/

This site offers links to online pre-Revolutionary Russian history books and Web sites.

British History Online. http://www.british-history.ac.uk/subject
.aspx?

This site contains primary and secondary written sources for
the medieval and modern history of England, Scotland, and
Wales. Browse by subject, place, period, or region.

EuroDocs: Online Sources for European History. http://eudocs.lib
.byu.edu/index.php/Main_Page

This site provides links to Western European historical documents, including facsimiles, transcriptions, and translations,
from ancient Europe to the present. Documents are organized
by country and period.

EyeWitness to History. http://www.eyewitnesstohistory.com

This site includes excerpts from primary sources, including
texts, photographs, and audio and film clips. Covers ancient
history to the twentieth century.

History World. www.historyworld.net

This site contains more than four hundred historical articles
searchable by time period, topic, and location. Timelines
provide links to over 10,000 world events. Also includes an
encyclopedia of Britain with more than five thousand entries
from AA to Zulu War.

Internet History Sourcebooks Project. http://www.fordham.edu/
halsall/index.html

This site provides access to public domain and copy-
permitted historical texts. There are three main sourcebooks
devoted to ancient, medieval, and modern history, and sub-
sidiary sourcebooks on topics such as African, Indian, Jewish,
and women's history.

NetSERF: The Internet Connection for Medieval Resources. http://
www.netserf.org/

This site provides links to sites on various aspects of medieval
life, including history, arts, culture, literature, music, religion,
and women. Includes the "largest general medieval glossary
on the Internet."

Portals to the World. http://www.loc.gov/rr/international/portals
.html

> This Library of Congress site provides links to worldwide
> online resources, with information on history, politics, and
> culture arranged by country or geographic area.

Proceedings of the Old Bailey. http://www.oldbaileyonline.org/

> This site allows access to roughly 200,000 trials held at the
> Old Bailey, London's central criminal court, from 1674 to
> 1913 and includes biographical details of approximately
> 2,500 people who were executed at Tyburn.

Repositories of Primary Sources. http://www.uiweb.uidaho.edu/
special-collections/Other.Repositories.html

> This site lists more than five thousand links to Web sites that
> house primary source materials for the study of North Ameri-
> can and world history.

Slave-studies.net. http://www.slave-studies.net/

> This site provides links to Internet resources pertaining to the
> global history of slavery and abolition from ancient times to
> the present.

A Teacher's Guide to the Holocaust. http://fcit.usf.edu/holocaust

> Organized into three categories (Timeline, People, and The
> Arts), this site includes links to primary and secondary
> sources related to the Holocaust, including documents, films,
> photographs, art, music, and literature.

Directories to online library catalogs

LibWeb. http://sunsite.berkeley.edu/Libweb

> This site lists online library servers in 146 countries, search-
> able by name, type, or country. It is updated daily.

WorldCat. http://www.worldcat.org/

> This site describes itself as "the world's largest network of
> library content and services." It provides links to over 10,000
> libraries and helps the user locate a title in nearby libraries.

Journal indexes

The vast majority of journal abstract and full-text article
databases are available to libraries only by subscription
(from online library vendors such as EBSCO, Gale, Project
Muse, ProQuest, and Wilson) and to the members of those
libraries, with appropriate password authentication, due to
licensing restrictions. The following is a selected list of some
subscription-only journal abstract and full-text article databases; there are hundreds of additional databases. Access var-
ies greatly from library to library. Ask at your local library to
determine what is available to you.

America: History and Life. Santa Barbara, CA: ABC-CLIO, 1964–.

This index contains abstracts of articles on the history of the United States and Canada published throughout the world, as well as articles dealing with current U.S. culture. Includes book reviews and abstracts of dissertations.

FirstSearch. Dublin, OH: OCLC. http://www.oclc.org/firstsearch/

This online service provides abstracts and full-text articles (more than ten million) from dozens of subject databases. Information on the product is available at the link, but searching is available only at subscribing libraries. Many *First-Search* databases are linked to *WorldCat*, the world's largest database of items held in libraries.

Historical Abstracts. Santa Barbara, CA: ABC-CLIO, 1955–.

This index contains abstracts from periodical literature covering world history from 1450. The scope excludes the United States and Canada. From 1971, it selectively indexes book reviews, monographs, and dissertations as well as periodical literature.

Humanities Full-Text. New York: H. W. Wilson, 1995–.

This index provides full-text articles from international magazines and journals in the field of humanities, including history, from 1995 onward. Indexing of articles dates back to 1984.

JSTOR: The Scholarly Journal Archive. http://www.jstor.org/

This online service for archiving academic journals provides abstracts and full-text articles from more than one thousand journals, some going as far back as the 1600s. *JSTOR* does not offer access to the most recent issues of journals. Information on the product is available at the link, but searching is available only at subscribing libraries.

Project Muse. http://muse.jhu.edu/

This index provides online access to more than four hundred journals in the humanities, arts, and social sciences. Indexing to article citations is available free at the above link. Online full-text articles are available at subscribing libraries and through interlibrary loan. *Project Muse* keeps an archive of its journals once they go online but does not have issues that predate them. In many cases, older articles are still useful, and students will need to find them by using print indexes.

Electronic (online) journals and magazines

An increasing number of periodicals (i.e., journals and magazines) are available in electronic format on the Internet. Your library may subscribe to online versions of print journals and periodicals through subscription-only online databases. Some periodicals offer free online access to entire issues, others provide access to selective articles, and others just list citations to the articles. These are a few sites to help you locate free (also called open-access) online periodicals and newspapers:

Directory of Open Access Journals. http://www.doaj.org/home

This directory offers access to more than 3,900 full-text journals; over 1,400 of these can be searched at the article level. Browse by journal title or search by subject.

The Internet Public Library: History. http://ipl.org/div/serials/ browse/hum30.00.00/ and http://www.ipl.org/div/subject/ browse/hum30.00.00/

These sites provide links to historical journals and magazines, primary source documents, and history blogs. Each URL returns different links.

The Internet Public Library: Newspapers Collection. http://www.ipl .org/div/news

This site lists online newspapers published worldwide. Search by title, geographical region, or country.

The Nineteenth-Century in Print: Periodicals. http://memory.loc .gov/ammem/ndlpcoop/moahtml/snchome.html.

Sponsored by the Library of Congress, American Memory Project, this site offers digital versions of twenty-three popular periodicals published between 1815 and 1901, including *Atlantic Monthly*, *North American Review*, and *Scientific American*.

Organizations

The following is a selected list of regional organizations:

American Historical Association. http://www.historians.org
Canada's National History Society. http://www.historysociety.ca/
H-Net. http://www.h-net.org
Oral History Association. http://www.oralhistory.org/
Organization of American Historians. http://www.oah.org/

For a more complete list of organizations, go to:

Google Directory. http://www.google.com/Top/Society/ Organizations/
The Internet Public Library: History. http://ipl.org/div/aon/browse/ hum30.00.00/

Index